Popular Mechanics

Router Fundamentals

Rick Peters

Hearst Books

A Division of Sterling Publishing Co., Inc.
New York

Produced by How-2 Media Inc.

Design: Triad Design Group

Cover Design: Celia Fuller

Photography: Christopher J. Vendetta

Contributing Writer: Cheryl A. Romano

Illustrations: Triad Design Group

Copy Editor: Barbara McIntosh Webb

Page Layout: Triad Design Group

Index: Nan Badgett

Every effort has been made to ensure that all information in this book is accurate. However, due to differing conditions, tools, and individual skills, the publisher cannot be responsible for injuries, losses, or other damages that may result from the use of information in this book.

Note: The safety guards were removed for clarity in many of the photographs in this book. Make sure to always use all safety devices according to the manufacturers' instructions.

Popular Mechanics Workshop: Router Fundamentals

Copyright © 2004 by Rick Peters

Library of Congress Cataloging-in-Publication Data Available.

10 9 8 7 6 5 4 3 2 1

Published by Hearst Books
A Division of Sterling Publishing Co., Inc.
387 Park Avenue South, New York, NY 10016

Popular Mechanics is a trademark owned by
Hearst Magazines Property, Inc., in USA, and
Hearst Communications, Inc., in Canada.
Hearst Books is a trademark owned by
Hearst Communications, Inc.

www.popularmechanics.com

Distributed in Canada by Sterling Publishing
C/o Canadian Manda Group, One Atlantic Avenue, Suite 105
Toronto, Ontario, Canada M6K 3E7

Distributed in Australia by Capricorn Link (Australia) Pty. Ltd.
P.O. Box 704, Windsor, NSW 2756 Australia

Printed in China

ISBN 1-58816-365-2

Contents

Acknowledgments   4

Introduction   5

Choosing a Router   6

Router Accessories   22

Handheld Router Techniques   46

Table-Mounted Router Techniques   86

Shop-Made Router Jigs & Fixtures   128

Maintenance & Troubleshooting   162

Router Projects   176

Index   190

Metric Equivalency Chart   192

ACKNOWLEDGMENTS

For all their help, advice, and support, I offer special thanks to:

Christopher Vendetta, ace photographer, for taking great photos with tight deadlines and in less than desirable conditions (my dusty workshop).

Jim Brewer and Lisa Agostoni of Freud Tools for supplying photos, technical data, and their high-quality router table, router fence, plunge router, and super-safe router bits.

Karen Slatter at Bench Dog for supplying technical information and images as well as their sturdy and easy-to-use router table, router tops, and router plates.

Karla Morely with Porter-Cable for supplying photos, technical information, and their nifty cordless router.

Doug Hicks with August Home Publishing for providing the photos of the ShopNotes router tables and Woodsmith aluminum box-joint jig.

David Olsen at Black & Decker for supplying images, technical information, and their affordable and easy-to-use plunge router.

Todd Walter with DeWalt Tools for providing images, technical information, and a couple of their well-crafted routers.

Leigh Bailey with Hitachi for supplying images, technical information, and two of their reliable routers.

Buddy Rohr with Sioux Tools for providing images, technical information, and one of their industrial-quality air-powered routers.

Richard Peterson at Milwaukee Electric Tool Corporation for supplying technical information and images of their routers.

Rob Lembo and the staff at Triad Design Group, for their superb illustrations and page layout talents that are evident in every page of this book.

Barb Webb, copyediting whiz, for ferreting out mistakes and gently suggesting corrections.

Heartfelt thanks to my constant inspiration: Cheryl, Lynne, Will, and Beth, for putting up with the craziness that goes with writing a book and living with a woodworker: late nights, wood everywhere, noise from the shop, and sawdust footprints in the house.

INTRODUCTION

Ask a group of experienced woodworkers what single portable power tool had the largest impact on their wood-working ability, and odds are that most will answer the router. No other tool brings such a wealth of woodworking techniques to hand as the router. Imagine a whole new world of woodworking techniques at your fingertips with the addition of a single tool. What's really great is that with the aid of some simple jigs that we'll show you how to make, you can rout with extreme precision and repeatability.

In these pages, you'll discover that a portable router is capable of routing decorative profiles on edges, capable of cutting grooves, dadoes, and rabbets for simple joinery, and with the aid of a jig or two, capable of routing perfect circles and cutting complex dovetails. By going a step further and mounting a router in a table, you'll be able to increase your repertoire of joinery skills by adding box joints, mortise-and-tenons, cope-and-stick-joints – even raised panels. Additional tricks include making your own dowels, using the router as a jointer, and turning your router into a duplicating machine with the aid of a pin arm.

We'll start by wading through the various types of routers available and show you what to look for in a router – and what to look out for – whether you're buying your first or thinking about upgrading to another. Then we'll take you through the myriad accessories you can purchase to make your router even more versatile. This is followed by hand-held and table-mounted techniques and a chapter of easy-to-make router jigs. To keep your new or old router running true, there's an entire chapter devoted to maintenance: everything from cleaning and adjusting bit-height mechanisms to sharpening router bits. Included in the final chapter are projects you can build that showcase a variety of techniques described in the book. We're sure that you'll want to hurry off to the shop after you've paged through this book.

Enjoy your woodworking, and make sure to follow all tool manufacturers' safety warnings.

—Joe Oldham
Editor-in-Chief, Popular Mechanics

1 Choosing a Router

The router is undoubtedly one of the most versatile tools in the woodworking shop. It can profile edges, make complicated joinery, create beautiful inlays — even joint wood. So how do you choose the router that's right for you? You start by learning all you can about the different types of routers and their features. That's what this chapter is all about. We'll take you through the basics and show what features to look for, and what to look out for: simple things like collet size and height-adjustment mechanisms that can make using your new router a joy or a chore. And, we'll demystify power ratings and make some recommendations.

Then it's up to you to try to match these up with what you plan to do with your router. Are you going to mount it in a table? Concentrate on joinery? Do mostly trim carpentry work? You need to answer these questions before choosing a router. There are more questions: Plunge or fixed-base? How much power do you need? What kinds of accessories are important? Combine your answers with our recommendations to find the router best suited to you.

With motor sizes ranging from 4.4 amps up to 15 amps, you can find a router to match just about any job in the shop. Each of the three basic router types is shown here: laminate trimmers, fixed-base routers, and plunge routers.

Router Types

Although there are dozens of different routers to choose from, they all fall into two basic categories: fixed-base routers or plunge routers, as shown in the photo below right.

This type of router excels at cutting mortises and is regarded by many as the tool of choice for mounting in a router table (see page 36), as the depth-of-cut adjustment is more accessible and easier to adjust. If you're planning on mounting the router in a table, consider buying at least a 3-hp model with variable speed. You'll be glad you have the extra power when using large profile bits that remove a lot of wood, such as vertical panel-raising bits.

Fixed-base

A fixed-base router consists of a router base and motor unit (at left in photo). The motor unit slides up and down or rotates within the base to adjust the depth of cut. Most fixed-base routers are single-speed and, because they have fewer parts than a plunge router, are generally more reliable. Many woodworkers prefer a fixed-base router for handheld work because its diminutive size makes it easier to maneuver. A $1^{1}/_{2}$-hp motor will handle most of the work you can throw at it. Look for easy, convenient adjustments and smooth, heavy-duty castings.

Plunge routers

Plunge routers are similar to fixed-base routers except that the motor unit slides up and down on a pair of spring-loaded metal rods (at right in photo above). The normal resting place of the motor unit is at the top of the rods. To make a cut, you release a lever and push down to lower (or plunge) the bit into the workpiece.

Fixed-Base Routers

A fixed-base router has two main parts: a motor housing and a base, see the drawing below left. The motor housing contains the motor and drive shaft to which the collet and/or collet nut attaches to accept a bit. It also contains the brush caps, which hold in the brushes. The on/off switch may or may not be in this unit, although it typically is. Speed controls range from simple on/off switches to electronic speed controls.

The router base accepts the motor housing and offers some type of height-adjustment mechanism, either a rack-and-pinion or a pin-and-groove system where a pin on the motor unit engages a spiral groove inside the router body. There's also some type of locking mechanism to secure the motor unit in the base once it has been adjusted to the desired depth of cut. This typically involves a split router base that squeezes or clamps the motor when the locking knob or lever is activated.

The bottom of the base is covered with a plastic sub-base that has an opening for the bit to pass through. This sub-base prevents the router from marring the surface of the workpiece. Handles on the side of the router provide the means to guide it during the cut. Most router bases have some type of depth-of-cut indicator, but this should be used only for rough positioning — always make a test cut to sneak up on the final cut.

ANATOMY OF A FIXED-BASE ROUTER

Speed Control Dial

On/Off Switch

Base Clamp Lever

Sub-Base

Motor Housing

Motor Alignment Arrow

Base

Chip Deflector

Collet

Template Guide Quick-Change Lever

Plunge Routers

Unlike most fixed-base routers, which have two separable parts (the motor and base), the parts of a plunge router do not come apart. The motor unit rides up and down on spring-loaded columns affixed to the base, see the drawing at right. The motor unit's resting position is at the top of the columns. When the plunge lever is released, the unit can be lowered and locked in place. Because of this sliding motion, the columns must be kept clean. Some manufacturers cover the columns with rubber sleeves, shaped like an accordion.

Plunge routers were used in production work for years mainly to rout mortises. Because of this, they tended to be large and powerful — 3-hp motors were common. Plunge routers today vary in size anywhere from 1-hp to 3-hp and larger. Because of the powerful, large motors, these routers tend to be awkward to use and when allowed to snap back to the rest position can often feel top-heavy.

Most plunge routers now offer advanced depth-of-cut capabilities. Unlike old production versions that were adjusted for a single plunge cut, newer models offer incremental adjustments that let you rout a mortise, for example, in three steps without having to stop and turn off the router (for more on this, see page 18). But even with stop rods, incremental stops, and hairline gauges, you should still make test cuts instead of relying on these to adjust the router for its final depth adjustment.

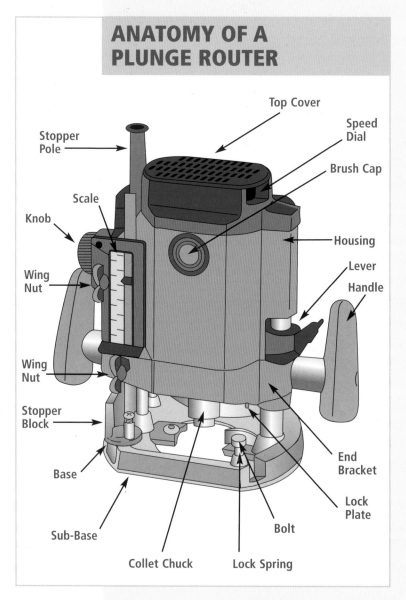

ANATOMY OF A PLUNGE ROUTER

- Top Cover
- Speed Dial
- Brush Cap
- Stopper Pole
- Scale
- Knob
- Housing
- Lever
- Handle
- Wing Nut
- Wing Nut
- Stopper Block
- End Bracket
- Base
- Lock Plate
- Sub-Base
- Bolt
- Collet Chuck
- Lock Spring

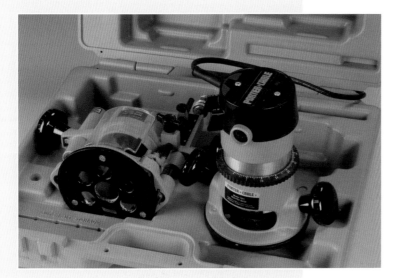

Dual-base routers

A popular trend in router manufacturing is router "kits" that offer a single motor unit and two bases: a fixed base and a plunge base (see the photo at left). Granted, this makes a lot of sense economically, but there are some drawbacks. First, the $1^{1}/_{2}$-hp motor units are usually designed for the fixed-base router in the kit. The problem is, you may find this unit is underpowered as a plunge router, especially if you mount it in a router table.

If you're interested in one of these kits, it's well worth the effort to visit a tool store and check out the different versions. You'll find a huge variance in changeabilty — that is, how easy or difficult it is to swap bases. This can vary from a complicated bar wedge that's tightened in the plunge router base to trap the motor unit in place, to simply screwing the router out of one base and into another. Don't let a sales clerk show you how easy it is to do this: Try out a couple of different systems for yourself.

CORDLESS ROUTERS

The only thing that's stopped routers from becoming cordless has been battery technology. Thankfully, recent advances have made this a reality (see the photo at right). The Porter-Cable router shown here uses a 19.2-volt battery that slides into place and locks positively.

If you've made the move from a corded to a cordless drill, you'll have some idea of how nice a cordless router can be to use. Years of ingrained habits will no longer be needed…habits like checking to make sure the power cord won't catch on the workpiece, on the clamps used to hold the workpiece in place, and on you.

As long as you take several lighter passes, which is generally the way to go (see page 53), this router has plenty of power to get through most jobs. Now naturally, you're not going to want to mount it under a router table — a corded router is still best for this. Once you go cordless, you'll wonder how you worked all those years with a corded unit.

Specialty Routers

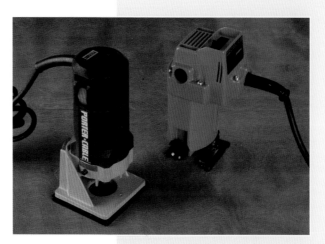

Laminate trimmers

Although originally intended only for trimming laminate edges on countertops, the compact size of laminate trimmers has made them a standard tool in many shops (photo at right). That's because they can get into places where larger routers just can't. For hand-held jobs, many woodworkers find themselves reaching for their laminate trimmer more regularly than their fixed-base router. The trimmers' low weight and powerful motors (these little guys have surprising torque) make them the perfect tool for a wide variety of routing challenges.

Like a fixed-base router, a laminate trimmer consists of two basic parts: a motor unit and a base (see the drawing at right). But because of the smaller size, everything is simpler. The motor unit has an on/off switch and functions as the handle. You simply wrap your hand around the unit and pull or push to rout. The motors are typically 5.6-hp and most run at 30,000 rpm.

Adjustment mechanisms are simple as well. Usually, a knurled knob is attached to a threaded stud that mates with threads on the side of the motor unit. Rotating the knob moves the unit up and down in the base. Another knurled knob locks the unit in place at the desired depth of cut. It's important to know that all laminate trimmers now on the market accept only $1/4$" bits. They were, after all, designed just to accept a flush-trim bit. Because of this you'll often find the bit opening too small to handle profiling bits, such as chamfers and round-overs. In cases like this, use your original base plate as a template to make a wood or acrylic plate that you can then enlarge the opening of, to handle these bits.

ANATOMY OF A LAMINATE TRIMMER

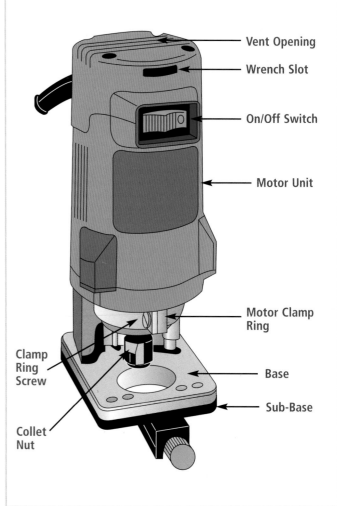

- Vent Opening
- Wrench Slot
- On/Off Switch
- Motor Unit
- Motor Clamp Ring
- Clamp Ring Screw
- Base
- Sub-Base
- Collet Nut

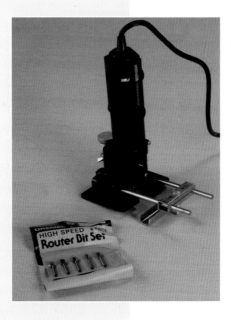

Dremel router

Another specialty router that you may find useful for detail work is the small Dremel router shown at left. Actually, it's just a Dremel tool fitted with a router attachment. A set of router bits is also available with $^1/_8$" shanks. The motor unit slips easily into the router base and is secured with a pair of screws. The router base comes standard with an edge guide, which makes it particularly useful for routing small grooves for intricate inlay. The tiny 1.15-amp motors on most Dremel tools either run at a fixed rate of 35,000 rpm or are variable from 5,000 to 35,000 rpm.

AIR-POWERED ROUTERS

Weighing in at less than 3 pounds and only $6^1/_2$" tall, you wouldn't think an air-powered router like the one shown below packs much punch. But you'd be wrong. Air-powered routers are the tools of choice in wood-related manufacturing environments for a couple of reasons. First, their small size coupled with plenty of power makes them easy to use. Second, because there's no motor, no windings, no brushes, not even an on/off switch to go bad, they're extremely reliable. What's more, there's no annoying whine of an electric motor, just the quiet hum of an air tool. The router shown here made by Sioux Tools (www.siouxtools.com) is $^3/_4$-hp and runs at 23,000 rpm. A $1^1/_2$-hp model is available as well as a laminate trimmer.

But an air-powered router isn't for everyone. Because they're designed for industrial use, they're expensive. And of all the air tools out there, routers require some of the largest air volumes to operate. Like most air tools, they run at 90 psi (pounds per square inch), but they require a lot of air movement or cfm (cubic feet per minute). For example, the $^3/_4$-hp router shown here needs around 20 cfm to run smoothly. Compressors that can produce this kind of airflow are usually 5-hp and above and require 220 volts to operate. Also, like any other air-powered tool, air routers work best with an in-line lubricator to keep the internal parts running smoothly. For woodworkers who use their air compressor for spraying finishes, this means adding a separate air line for the router to prevent the oil in the system from contaminating finishes.

Router Collets

Collet size

There are two main sizes of router collets. The size indicates the shank diameter of the router bit it can accept, typically $1/4$" or $1/2$" (left and right in the photo, respectively). Savvy router manufacturers are beginning to ship their routers with both collets because $1/2$"-shank bits are rapidly becoming the industry standard. Other manufacturers ship only a $1/2$" collet with a $1/4$" reducer. We recommend the stiffer $1/2$" bits, as they flex less and help reduce chatter and vibration. Note: You will occasionally come across a router with a $3/8$" collet, but bits are not commonly available for this size anymore, so they are increasingly rare.

Collet types

As far as collet types go, either the collet is split or the end of the motor shaft or arbor is split to grip the bit when the collet nut is tightened (left collet in top drawing). Split collets can have a single split (middle collet in top drawing) or be split into multiple segments (far right collet in top drawing). Basically, the greater the number of segments, the better and more uniformly the collet will grip a bit. A nifty version of the multi-segmented collet is the auto-release collet. These collets will release a bit once the collet nut is loosened fully — no more stuck bits. The segmented collet is best: When it wears out, it's simple (though surprisingly expensive) to replace. When a split shaft wears out, you basically need a new router. (For more on maintaining collets, see pages 166–167.)

Proper grip

Regardless of the size or type of collet, it's important to know that there's a right and a wrong way to install a bit in a collet. In order for the collet to grip the bit as securely as possible, router and router bit manufacturers recommend that the bit's shank should

not bottom out in the collet (bottom drawing). Manufacturers further suggest that this lessens vibration transferred to the bit. Also, at least three-fourths of the bit's shank should be gripped in the collet. Any less, and you run the risk of the bit working its way loose in use.

COLLET DESIGN

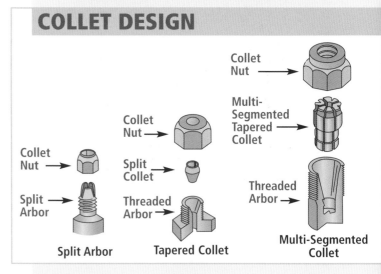

Collet Nut

Split Arbor

Split Collet

Threaded Arbor

Tapered Collet

Collet Nut

Multi-Segmented Tapered Collet

Threaded Arbor

Multi-Segmented Collet

GRIPPING A BIT PROPERLY

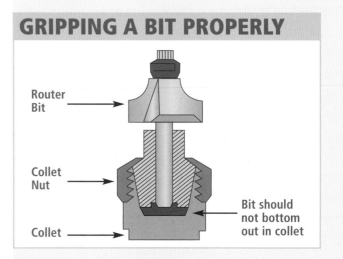

Router Bit

Collet Nut

Collet

Bit should not bottom out in collet

Motor Power

When shopping for a router, you'll find almost as many terms to describe power as there are router manufacturers. That's because there are no rules on how a manufacturer has to define power. The most commonly used term, though, is horsepower.

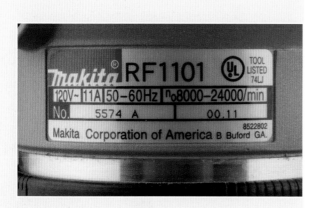

Horsepower

Horsepower is the amount of work done over time. It's defined as a unit of power equal in the United States to 746 watts or the amount of energy required to lift 550 pounds up 1 foot in 1 second. Generally, when used to describe a tool, like a router, horsepower is an indication of how capable of performing its tasks the router is. The rated horsepower (hp) of a router is usually the torque level at which the motor can be run continuously without exceeding the temperature at which the winding insulation breaks down.

What this means is that you can get a higher hp from a router for short periods. The risk you run is damaging your router. Running a router harder than it's rated for will cause the motor windings to heat up. When a router bogs down, it will pull more current trying to keep the speed constant. But the windings aren't designed to handle this extra current; they'll heat up and eventually melt.

Amperage rating

Although most toolmakers continue to describe their products in terms of horsepower, the true indicator of a tool's power is its amperage rating. As a rule of thumb, the higher the amperage, the more powerful the tool is. Amperage ratings can be found on the router's motor label, as seen in the photo above left. Disregard meaningless marketing labels, such as "heavy-duty" or "industrial," that are often used to supposedly indicate how powerful a router is.

"DEVELOPS" HORSEPOWER

No motor produces usable horsepower unless it is slowed down by applying a mechanical load. Unscrupulous vendors sometimes publish maximum "developed" horsepower to make their products seem more capable than they really are. Developed horsepower may be 2 to 5 times the continuous-duty rating of a motor. The phrase "develops 3 hp" is meaningless marketing hype — stick with the amperage rating.

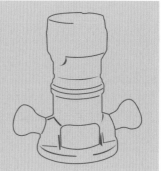

Ergonomics

We always recommend that tool shoppers get their hands on a potential tool before buying it. This is the only way to determine whether the tool's ergonomics and your hands are a good match: Grip the tool, turn the power switch on and off, change a bit or two, play with the height adjustment, etc. There are two ergonomic features that will greatly affect how comfortable any given router is for you to use: handle type and location, and the type and location of the on/off switch.

Power switch

An important feature to look for in a router is how accessible the on/off switch is. Look at the routers in the top photo, from left to right. On the first router, the on/off trigger is on top of the motor housing. The second router's on/off switch is a toggle switch on the side of the motor housing above one of the handles. The switch on the third router is lower on the motor's housing and can be flipped on or off with a thumb without releasing a handle. Likewise, the large toggle switch on the last router is located directly above the handle and is designed for thumb operation while still gripping the handle.

Handles

For portable use, handle type and placement are big deals. It's not so important when a router is mounted in a table. (Note: The handles on many larger routers, particularly plunge routers, will need to be removed in order to pass through the opening in the table top.) There are three basic types of handle configurations: round or roundish knobs low down on the sides of the router, most common on fixed-base routers (photo A at right); larger rectangular handles higher on the sides, usually found on plunge routers (photo B at right); and a D-handle configuration common on production routers (photo C at right).

Fixed-Base Router Adjustments

The critical adjustment on a router is bit height or depth of cut and its locking mechanism. Since you'll be constantly adjusting bit height, it makes sense to find a router with a mechanism that's both precise and comfortable to use. Fixed-base routers use one of three basic systems: rack and pinion, pin and groove, and a version of pin and groove called collar and groove.

Bit-height adjustment

Rack-and-pinion height adjustments were common on older routers (far left router in photo below). Although precise, the fine teeth of both the rack and the pinion quickly fill with dust and become hard to operate. If cleaned religiously, however, they work well, but take time to adjust from one end of the range to the other. Pin-and-collar adjustment mechanisms have become the standard on most fixed-base routers (far right router in photo). A pin on the side of the motor unit tracks in a spiral groove in the base housing. To adjust height, you simply rotate the motor unit. This type of mechanism adjusts quickly but is not very precise, as there's typically quite a bit of slop between the pin and the groove.

To eliminate this problem, a variation called a collar and groove was designed (middle router in photo). This system employs a wider groove and a larger pin, which is part of the molded plastic collar that rests on top of the base. The plastic pin fits snugly in the widened groove and provides more precise adjustment. But regardless of the system, height adjustments should be considered rough placement. Always make a test cut to verify bit height, and readjust as necessary.

Locking mechanism

Virtually all fixed-base routers have a split lower case. The split is spanned by some type of locking mechanism that, when activated, pulls the two halves together to pinch the motor unit and lock it in place. In the router in the middle of the above left photo, the locking mechanism is an easy-to-use snap-type lever. On the router to its right, the locking mechanism is a paddle-style bolt in the rear of the router. Most woodworkers find the snap-lever easier to operate and more convenient. The only way you'll know is to give it a try.

Plunge Router Adjustments

Plunge routers adjust the bit height via the plunge rods and the locking lever; multiple height stops are available on some units (see below). Almost all plunge routers have a depth adjustment scale and depth stop rod on the side of the housing.

Bit height

Bit height on a plunge router can be adjusted two ways: by releasing the locking lever and pushing the router down to the desired depth of cut and then engaging the locking lever, or by adding a fine-adjustment control knob to the threaded depth stop rod (far left router in photo at right). Locking levers are conveniently located behind one of the router handles so you can operate it without letting go of the router handle. Depth of cut is quick this way, but hard to fine-adjust. The depth stop and scale is used by loosening a thumbscrew or knob, allowing the stop rod to slide up and down. After the rod is located for the desired depth, the knob is tightened. In use, the motor unit is plunged down for the cut and will stop when the rod hits the base at the desired depth.

Multiple stops

Plunge router manufacturers are aware of problems with adjusting bit height, and in response have added incremental stops below the depth stop rod. These tiny turrets pivot to locate one of three adjustable stops under the stop rod (photo at right). For example, if you adjust these in thirds, you can rout a mortise in three passes by pivoting the turret without having to turn off the router. A control knob makes fine adjustments easy but can be tiring when you need to adjust a bit from one extreme to another (for more on plunge router handles, see page 41). Fine-control knobs are an absolute necessity for a plunge router mounted in a table.

Changing Router Bits

Changing bits on a router should be as easy as changing bits on a drill or drill press. But it isn't, because the collet on a router isn't as accessible as a drill's chuck. On plunge routers, the plunge rods are in the way. With a fixed-base router, the lower housing partially wraps around the collet to limit access. Additionally, the method used to loosen and tighten the collet can affect how hard or easy it is to change bits. There are two common methods: a stop and a single wrench, or two wrenches.

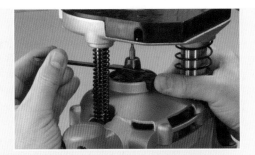

Stop and a single wrench

It's really a matter of personal preference whether you like routers that use a stop and a single wrench. Note: This method is becoming increasingly popular on plunge routers. With this method, either a pin or a metal bar is pushed in with one hand to capture the collet and stop it from rotating (top photo at left). Then you can loosen or tighten the collet with a single wrench. The problem with this system is it often locks the collet in a position where you can't fit the wrench on the collet nut because it's oriented incorrectly. You'll find yourself often having to release the lock and rotate the collet manually to find a position where you can get the wrench on the nut. This is not a big problem, but it can get annoying over time.

No stop, two wrenches

The prevailing method used to tighten and loosen collets is with two wrenches and no stop. One wrench is placed on the motor shaft or arbor, the other on the collet nut. Here again, access can be a problem. This is easily solved on fixed-base routers with a pin-and-groove adjustment mechanism: Just spin the motor unit out of the base house, and you've got total access (photo at left). Be careful not to overtighten the collet, as this can cause it to fail prematurely (see the sidebar below).

ONE-HANDED OPERATION

Many woodworkers struggle with the wrenches used to tighten and loosen most router collets. Typically they'll take a wrench in each hand and, with Popeye-like effort, tighten the collet or break it free and rap their knuckles together. The best way to avoid this is to use just one hand. Place one wrench on the spindle and the other on the collet so the wrenches are splayed slightly. Then squeeze to loosen or tighten (as shown in the photo). The pressure from one hand is all you should ever need to hold a bit. If more is required, it's time to replace the collet.

■ RECOMMENDATIONS

What's the best router to buy? It all depends on how you plan on using the router: mainly as a handheld, or mounted in a table? Most woodworkers find that a fixed-base router or a laminate trimmer is better suited for handheld work and a plunge router works best as a table-mounted router. If you can afford it, buy both. If not, some manufacturers offer router kits (see page 11) consisting of a fixed-base router with an optional base that converts it into a plunge router. With this setup, you can mount the plunge base in your router table and keep the fixed base on hand for handheld work. It's important here to find a motor unit that's quick and easy to move from one base to another. The type that unscrews in and out works best here.

One of the primary features to decide on when purchasing a router is whether or not you need plunge capability. There are three good reasons to go with plunge routers over fixed-base routers: They let you safely make plunge cuts (such as when routing mortises), they're easier to adjust, and they're handier in a router table. If you're not planning on mounting the router in a table and you have no intention of routing mortises, a fixed-base router will serve you well; otherwise, a plunge router is your best bet.

As far as power is concerned, a 1½-hp single-speed fixed-base router will handle most any job. For table-mounted routers, consider stepping up to at least a 3-hp router with variable speed. This will allow

FIXED-BASE ROUTERS

Manufacturer	Model #	Amps	HP	No-Load RPM	Collet
Bosch	1617	11.0	1¾	25,000	¼"–½"
	1617EVS	12.0	2	8,000–25,000	¼"–½"
Craftsman	17510	8.5	1½	25,000	¼"
	26834	9.5	2	15,000–25,000	¼"–½"
DeWalt	DW610	9.0	1½	25,000	¼"–½"
	DW616	11.0	1¾	24,500	¼"–½"
	DW618	12.0	2¼	8,000–24,000	¼"–½"
Dremel	275	1.15	n/a	35,000	⅛"
	395	1.15	n/a	5,000–35,000	⅛"
Makita	3606	7.0	1	30,000	¼"
		11.0	2¼	8,000–24,000	¼"–½"
Milwaukee	5619-20	11.0	1¾	24,000	¼"–½"
	5625-20	15.0	3½	10,000–22,000	¼"–½"
Porter-Cable	690	10.0	1½	23,000	¼"–½"
	7536	13.0	2½	21,000	¼"–½"
	7518	15.0	3¼	10,000–21,000*	¼"–½"
Ryobi	R161K	8.0	1½	25,000	¼"
Skil	1810-01	9.0	1¾	25,000	¼"
	1815-04	10.0	2	25,000	¼"

* five speeds: 10,000, 13,000, 16,000, 19,000, and 21,000 rpm

LAMINATE TRIMMERS

Manufacturer	Model #	Description	Amps	No-Load RPM
Bosch	1608	Trim router	5.6	30,000
	1608T	Tilt-base	5.6	30,000
	1690A	Offset-base	5.6	30,000
Craftsman	27512	Trim router	3.8	23,000
DeWalt	DW670	Trim router	5.6	30,000
Hitachi	TR6	Trimmer	4.0	30,000
Makita	3707FC	Fixed-base	4.4	26,000
	3708FC	Tilt-base	4.4	26,000
Porter-Cable	7310	Trimmer	5.6	30,000
	7312	Offset-base	5.6	30,000
	7319	Tilt-base	5.6	30,000
Ryobi	TR31	Trim router	3.8	23,000

you to vary the speed as needed for larger bits and different wood species.

Finally, make sure a router you're considering has a $1/2$" collet — it's rapidly becoming the industry standard. Just as no one is making 8-tracks for your old 8-track player, you eventually won't find $1/4$" bits. The stouter $1/2$" shanks run truer, offering vibration-free, clean cuts. Most manufacturers provide both $1/4$" and $1/2$" collets with their routers, or more recently, a $1/2$" collet with a $1/4$" reducer insert.

PLUNGE ROUTERS

Manufacturer	Model #	Amps	HP	No-Load RPM	Collet Size	Plunge Capacity
Black & Decker	RP200	9.0	$1^3/4$	25,000	$1/4$"	2"
	RP400K	10.0	2	8,000–25,000	$1/4$"	2"
Bosch	1613AEVS	11.0	2	12,000–22,000	$1/4$"–$1/2$"	2-$1/8$"
	1619EVS	15.0	$3^1/4$	12,000–23,000	$1/4$"–$1/2$"	2$9/16$"
Craftsman	26835	15.0	3	23,000	$1/4$"–$1/2$"	2$1/2$"
DeWalt	DW621	10.0	2	8,000–24,000	$1/4$"–$1/2$"	2$1/8$"
	DW625	15.0	3	8,000–22,000	$1/4$"–$1/2$"	2$7/16$"
Freud	FT2000E	15.0	$3^1/4$	8,000–22,000	$1/4$"–$1/2$"	2$3/4$"
Hitachi	M8V	7.3	$1^1/2$	10,000–25,000	$1/4$"	2"
	M12V	15	$3^1/4$	8,000–20,000	$1/4$"–$1/2$"	2$7/16$"
	TR12	12.2	3	22,000	$1/4$"–$1/2$"	2$3/8$"
Makita	3612	15.0	$3^1/4$	9,000–23,000	$1/4$"–$1/2$"	2$3/8$"
	3621	7.8	$1^1/4$	24,000	$1/4$"	1$3/8$"
	RP1101	11	$2^1/4$	8,000–24,000	$1/4$"–$1/2$"	2$19/32$"
Porter-Cable	693	10.0	$1^1/2$	23,000	$1/4$"–$1/2$"	2$1/2$"
	7538	15.0	$3^1/4$	21,000	$1/2$"	3"
	7539	15.0	$3^1/4$	10,000–21,000*	$1/4$"–$1/2$"	3"
Ryobi	RE180PL	10.0	2	15,000–23,000	$1/4$"–$1/2$"	2"
Skil	1820-04	10.0	2	25,000	$1/4$"	2"
	1845	10.0	2	8,000–25,000	$1/4$"	2"

* five speeds: 10,000, 13,000, 16,000, 19,000, and 21,000 rpm

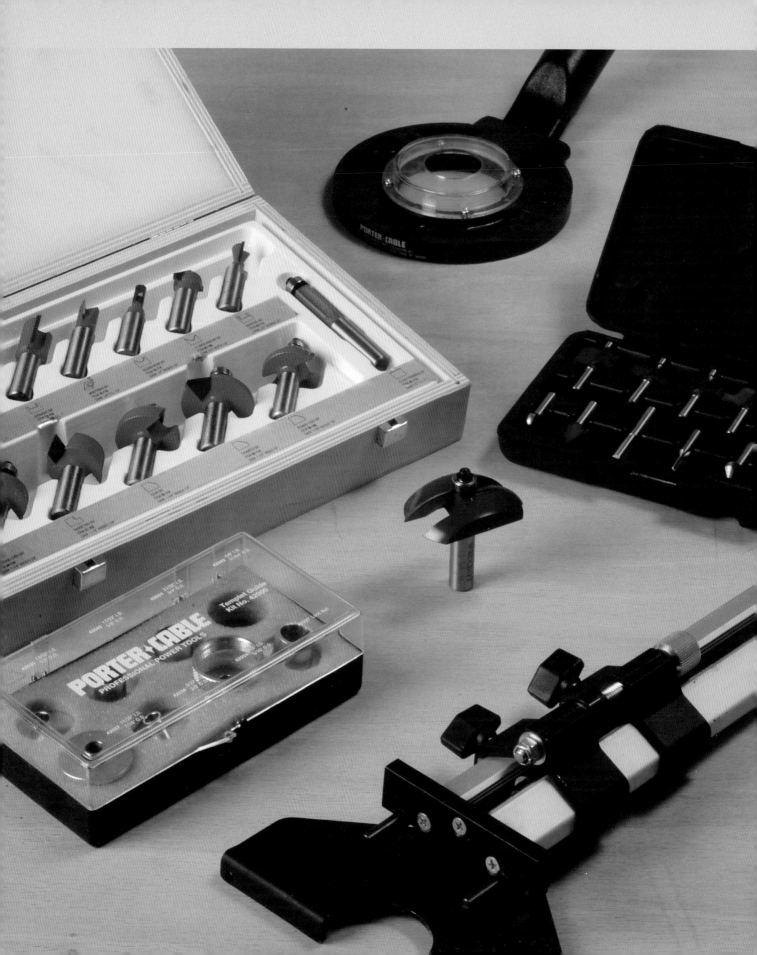

2 Router Accessories

Glance through any mail-order woodworking tools catalog and you'll find page after page of accessories for the router. This is just another testament to the versatility of this incredible tool. And every time a new catalog arrives, somebody has come up with yet another jig to use with a router.

The most common accessories are router bits. These are available in a huge selection of profiles, and come in either high-speed steel or carbide-tipped. Quality varies greatly, so it's a good idea to always buy from a name you trust.

Router add-ons range from simple edge guides to the ultimate router accessory: the router table, which basically turns a handheld router into a stationary shaper. Other specialty jigs such as circle-cutting jigs, horizontal mortisers, and dovetail jigs can further expand the capabilities of your router. You can purchase these, or make some yourself. See Chapter 5 on pages 128–161 for shop-made jigs and fixtures.

Want to cut circles with your router? Dovetails? All it takes are an accessory such as a circle or dovetail jig and the right bits. Router accessories allow you to craft precision box joinery, rout decorative edges, and even make your own custom moldings.

Router Bits

It's odd that router bits are classified as accessories. A router without a bit is like a computer without software — all you can do is plug it in and stare at it. There are two basic types of router bits available: unpiloted and piloted.

You'll also have a choice of shank size — either $1/4"$ or $1/2"$. If your router will accept $1/2"$ bits, by all means use them. The stouter shank of a $1/2"$ will not only stand up better over time, but the thicker shank also helps reduce both flexing and vibration to provide a much more accurate cut. A common problem with $1/4"$-shank bits, chattering, is virtually eliminated with $1/2"$-shank bits. Chattering is caused when the bit shank flexes and practically bounces along the edge of a workpiece as it cuts.

Both types of bits can be found made from high-speed steel, or HSS (at left in the photo at right), or with carbide tips (at right in the photo at right). As a general rule of thumb, you'll want to go with carbide. They cost more, but they'll stay sharper a whole lot longer. The single advantage (besides being less expensive) that HSS bits offer over carbide-tipped bits is that you can easily modify the profile of a high-speed steel bit if desired. This occasionally comes up with antique reproductions, where you might want to alter a bit to create a custom profile. If you do, make sure to change both profiles in an identical manner. Otherwise, one of the profiles will end up working harder than the other and will dull quickly.

CARBIDE THICKNESS

Not all carbide-tipped router bits are the same. When shopping for these bits, compare the thickness of the carbide tips. You may find less expensive bits with thinner carbide (at right in photo) compared to the thickness of a quality bit (at left in photo). A reputable manufacturer will always be able to identify how thick their carbide is.

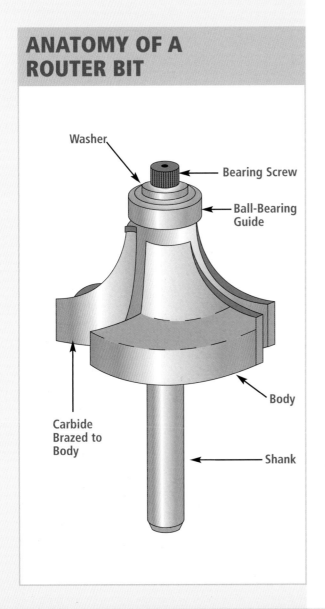

Washer

Bearing Screw

Ball-Bearing Guide

Carbide Brazed to Body

Body

Shank

Basic Bit Design

Let's take a close look at the basic design of a router bit. Quality bits are forged and then turned to the desired shape on a metal lathe. Slots or gullets are then cut to allow for chip clearance. On anti-kickback bits, these gullets are much smaller than on conventional bits (see page 26 for more on this.)

If the bit will be a piloted bit (that is, it uses a bearing to guide the cut), a hole will be drilled and tapped in the end of the bit. The end of the shank is chamfered slightly to make it easier to slip the bit into a collet. Next, two pieces of high-grade carbide are brazed to the body of the bit. The bit then goes off to the sharpening station, where the cutting portion of the carbide is ground to the exact profile, along with the desired shear angle. After the carbide is polished to its final edge, the bit moves along to assembly, where if necessary, a bearing washer, a bearing, and a bearing screw are installed.

Finally, the bit should undergo vigorous quality control testing (such as making sure it's perfectly balanced to minimize vibration) before it's shipped off to you or to the tool store.

INTERCHANGEABLE CUTTERS

One way to keep bit cost down is to design cutters that use an interchangeable arbor, like those shown in the photo at right. This may not seem like a bad idea, but it has some drawbacks. First, most of the cutters that fit on these arbors are conventional and not anti-kickback — and that makes them not as safe. Second, there's no way a cutter could be balanced for multiple arbors. This means you'll end up with more vibration, and cuts that aren't as clean as you'd like.

ANTI-KICKBACK BITS

A nti-kickback router bits are a fairly new breed of bits pioneered by Freud (www.freudinc.com). What makes these bits different from ordinary router bits is the large body that wraps around in front of the cutter (far left in the photo at right).

This design limits the amount of cut under unsafe conditions, such as if you were to slip and push a workpiece into a spinning bit (see the middle drawing at right). With a conventional bit (like the middle and far right bit in the photo above right), the cutter would slam into the workpiece, take a huge bite, and fling the workpiece back at you. This nasty event is called kickback (see the drawing below).

With an anti-kickback bit, the workpiece would hit the large body in front of the bit and take a much smaller bite, and the kickback (if any) would be greatly reduced. These work so well that many woodworkers have replaced their conventional bits with anti-kickback bits.

Yes, quality anti-kickback bits do cost more than conventional bits. But can you put a price on your fingers? One kickback incident is all it takes to drag your hand or fingers into a spinning bit. Of course, you can hurt yourself with an anti-kickback bit if you stick your finger into a spinning bit. The big difference is that the wound will be much less severe than if you got nipped by a conventional bit.

ANTI-KICKBACK DESIGN

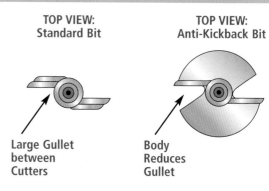

TOP VIEW: Standard Bit

TOP VIEW: Anti-Kickback Bit

Large Gullet between Cutters

Body Reduces Gullet

HOW ANTI-KICKBACK BITS WORK

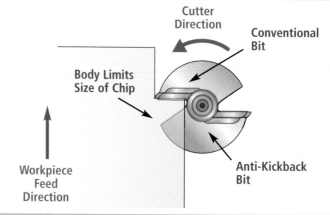

Cutter Direction

Conventional Bit

Body Limits Size of Chip

Anti-Kickback Bit

Workpiece Feed Direction

Bit Types

There are two basic bit types: piloted and non-piloted. A piloted bit is any router bit that has a built-in guide. Most bits that are used to rout a decorative edge are piloted bits: round-over bits, cove bits, chamfer bits, and ogee bits, to name a few. The most common type of guide used today is the bearing. A bearing is mounted either below or above the cutter and is pressed against the edge of the workpiece. The bearing rides along the edge of the workpiece (or template) to guide the cutter (see the photo at left).

The width of cut of some bits can be changed by replacing the bearing with a different size or by changing a rub collar (see the sidebar below) to a smaller diameter. This is especially common with rabbeting bits so that you can cut a variety of rabbet widths with the same bit. Almost all of the bearings used on bits today are sealed bearings, and it's important to be careful when cleaning these bits. Although they're sealed, solvents typically used to clean bits can still seep into the bearing, causing the bearing grease to dissolve and break down. Make sure to always remove a bearing before cleaning a bit; pages 173–174 cover bit maintenance.

BEARING VERSUS NON-BEARING GUIDED BITS

When piloted router bits first hit the market many years ago, the guide was simply a rub collar that was either machined as part of the bit (at left in photo) or a separate part that threaded into the bottom of the bit. Unfortunately, when the collar was pressed against the edge of the workpiece to guide the cut, it often burned, glazed, or dimpled the edge of the wood. So, savvy bit manufacturers developed the bearing-guided bit (at right in photo). Today, practically all quality piloted bits feature bearings.

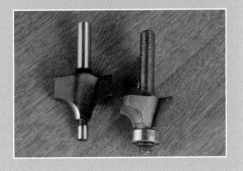

Common Bit Profiles

Piloted bits typically make up the bulk of most router bit collections. Probably the most common profile is the round-over. Round-over bits are available in radii ranging from a diminutive $1/8$" up to 1" and over for industrial applications. Beading bits are simply round-over bits with smaller bearings that allow for a deeper cut, resulting in a lip or bead. Common sizes are $1/4$", $3/8$", and $1/2$".

Decorative profiles such as the Roman ogee and reverse Roman ogee are commonly available with integral or bearing guides. Another useful profile is the cove. These bits range in sizes with radii from $1/4$" up to 1".

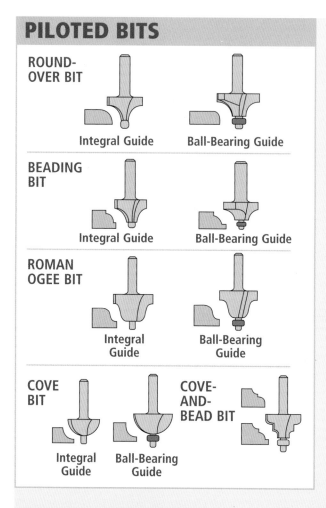

PILOTED BITS

ROUND-OVER BIT
Integral Guide   Ball-Bearing Guide

BEADING BIT
Integral Guide   Ball-Bearing Guide

ROMAN OGEE BIT
Integral Guide   Ball-Bearing Guide

COVE BIT
Integral Guide   Ball-Bearing Guide

COVE-AND-BEAD BIT

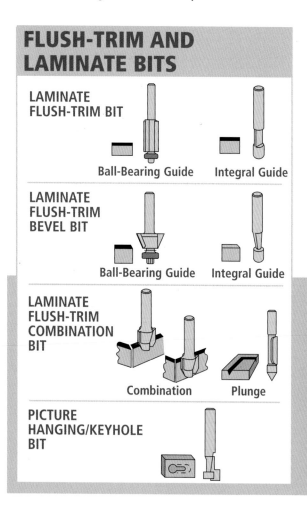

FLUSH-TRIM AND LAMINATE BITS

LAMINATE FLUSH-TRIM BIT
Ball-Bearing Guide   Integral Guide

LAMINATE FLUSH-TRIM BEVEL BIT
Ball-Bearing Guide   Integral Guide

LAMINATE FLUSH-TRIM COMBINATION BIT
Combination   Plunge

PICTURE HANGING/KEYHOLE BIT

FLUSH-TRIM BITS

Although most woodworkers have a single flush-trim bit in their bit case, flush-trim bits are available in a surprisingly wide variety of shapes and sizes. The major difference among these bits is the profile. Most are straight, but a number are beveled to cut a slight angle on the laminate. In addition, combination bits are available that can trim flush and add a bevel, or make a plunge cut and trim flush or at an angle.

Next to the round-over bit, the next most popular piloted bit is the rabbet or rabbeting bit, sized commonly from $1/4$" up to 1". Many rabbeting bits come with bearings that are not removable. Others are made so you can remove the bearing and replace it with a larger or smaller bearing to cut varying size rabbets.

Pattern-cutting or patternmaker's bits are a variation of the flush-trim bit. Instead of the bearing being located on the bottom of the bit, it's located on top near the shank. Both of these bits are ideal for patternmaking (see page 79 for more on this technique).

The other bit you're most likely to see in a collection is the chamfer bit. These bits usually come in only one size — all you need do is vary the depth of cut to produce different size chamfers. The one thing that can vary from bit to bit is the cutter angle. Typical angles include 45 degrees, 30 degrees, and $22^1/2$ degrees.

Other decorative profiles you may find useful are edge-beading bits and what are called "classic" pattern bits. The profile of a classic pattern bit will vary from manufacturer to manufacturer.

MORE PILOTED BITS

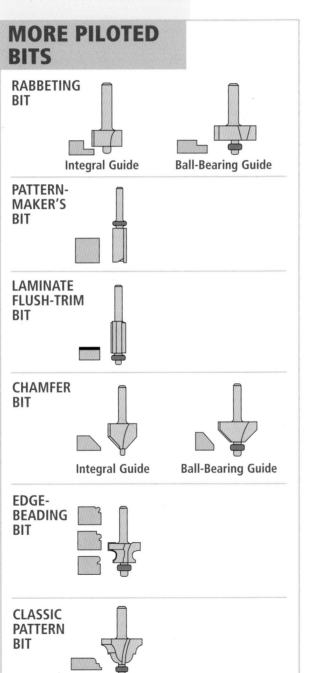

RABBETING BIT

Integral Guide   Ball-Bearing Guide

PATTERN-MAKER'S BIT

LAMINATE FLUSH-TRIM BIT

CHAMFER BIT

Integral Guide   Ball-Bearing Guide

EDGE-BEADING BIT

CLASSIC PATTERN BIT

Non-Piloted Bits

An unpiloted or non-piloted bit is any router bit that can make a cut in from the edge of a workpiece (see the photo at right). Since no means are provided to guide the bit, it can be used either freehand (such as when routing a name in a sign) or with the aid of an edge guide or straightedge (see pages 61–62 for more on this).

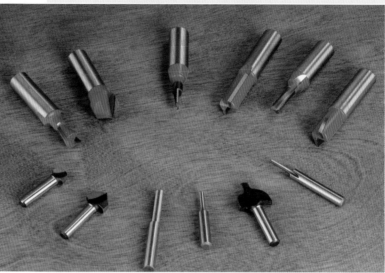

The most common type of non-piloted bits are straight bits. These are one of the workhorse bits used for cutting grooves, dadoes, rabbets, and myriad joints such as the locking rabbet, box joint, and mortise-and-tenon. Straight bits are typically available in sizes ranging from $1/8$" up to 1" in diameter. They also come in single flute and double flute designs. Although you can make a plunge cut with any straight bit, special bits with angled ends are designed specifically for this task. When chip clearance is an issue, such as when routing mortises, a special type of straight bit called a spiral flute bit is used. The flutes are similar to those on a twist bit and are engineered to either pull chips up and out or push them down and out.

By modifying the end of a straight bit you get a veining or grooving bit. The ends of these bits are rounded over and are used to rout decorative grooves and flutes. Mortising or hinge-mortising bits are also modified straight bits: They look just like them, except the cutters are often shorter than on a conventional straight bit.

Core-box bits and V-groove bits are non-piloted bits used primarily for routing decorative grooves. The core-box bit routs a full half-circle instead of a quarter-circle as a cove bit does. Likewise, the V-groove bit can rout a full triangle-shaped groove instead of the half-triangle that a chamfer bit can produce.

PROFILES OF NON-PILOTED BITS

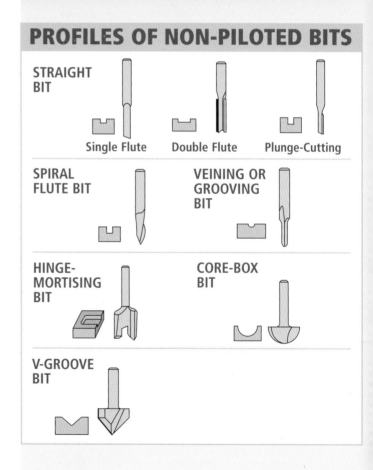

STRAIGHT BIT
— Single Flute — Double Flute — Plunge-Cutting

SPIRAL FLUTE BIT

VEINING OR GROOVING BIT

HINGE-MORTISING BIT

CORE-BOX BIT

V-GROOVE BIT

Additional decorative non-piloted bits are beading bits, classic pattern bits, and ogee bits. These are most often used for making decorative moldings for picture frames, custom trim, and antique restoration work. Even more specialized are bits like the edge mold bit shown here, which is designed to cut a specific design on the edge of a workpiece. Bits like this are most often found in the bit cabinets of woodworkers who make custom cabinetry.

Dovetail bits are available in a wide variety of sizes and angles. The old standby that most dovetail jigs use is the $1/2$" dovetail, as it will cut half-blind dovetails in $3/4$"-thick stock. Most dovetail jig manufacturers offer both dovetail and straight bits designed specifically for their jigs. For more on dovetail jigs and how to use them, see page 44 and pages 72–75, respectively.

There are also numerous additional joint-specific bits, like the locking-miter bit shown here, that cut one joint. A finger-joint bit and a glue-joint bit are just two other examples.

MORE NON-PILOTED BITS

BEADING BIT

CLASSIC PATTERN BIT

OGEE BIT

EDGE MOLD BIT

DOVETAIL BIT

LOCKING-MITER BIT

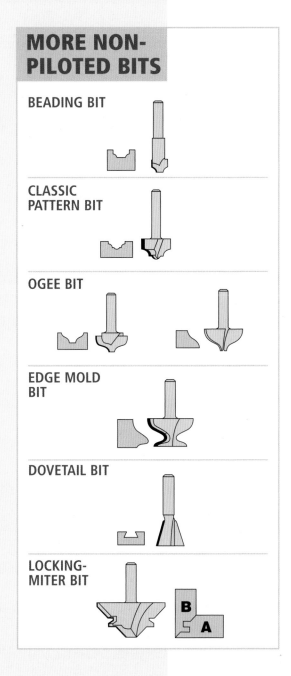

Specialty Bits

In addition to edge-profiling bits and standard non-piloted bits (such as straight bits), there are several router bits available designed to make special cuts.

A slot cutter is a piloted bit that allows you to easily rout slots or grooves in the edge of a workpiece. The advantage here is that the workpiece lies flat on the router table or workbench and gravity works for you instead of against you.

A keyhole bit routs a recessed slot for hanging pictures and cabinets. This is a non-piloted bit that requires some type of edge guide for a straight cut.

Cope-and-stick bit sets, often called rail-and-stile sets, are used to join the rails and stiles of a frame together. This joint is the predominant technique used to join the doors on most cabinets, especially kitchen cabinetry. These bits should always be purchased in matched sets. Each bit cuts a mirror image of the other. The cope (rail) bit is used only on the ends of the rails. The stick (stile) bit is used to rout a matching profile on the ends of the stiles as well as all inside edges of the frame. Not only does this create a molded edge detail, but it also cuts a groove in the edge for the frame's panel. For more on using a cope-and-stick bit set, see pages 116–117.

There are two basic types of bits for making raised panels: horizontal panel-raising bits

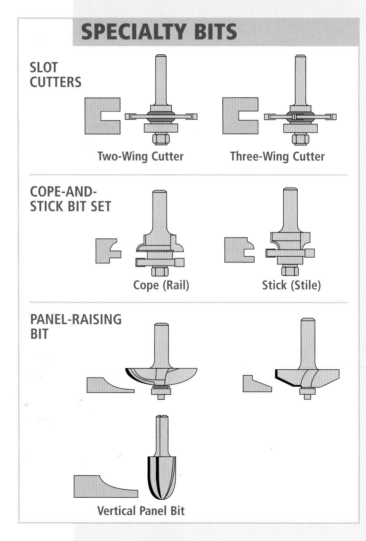

SPECIALTY BITS

SLOT CUTTERS

Two-Wing Cutter   Three-Wing Cutter

COPE-AND-STICK BIT SET

Cope (Rail)   Stick (Stile)

PANEL-RAISING BIT

Vertical Panel Bit

and vertical panel-raising bits. Both make a large scooped cut in the edges of the panel, and both remove a lot of wood. Horizontal panel-raising bits can be dangerous because so much of the cutterhead is exposed. A safer approach is the vertical bits (for more on creating a raised panel, see pages 118–119). Regardless of the orientation, panel-raising bits can be found in many different profiles. Because of the large cutterhead, these bits do tend to be quite expensive.

Safety Note: Panel-raising bits — regardless of the orientation — should never be used in a handheld router. They should *only* be installed in a table-mounted router. The cutterheads are simply too large to safely control in a handheld router.

MULTI-PROFILE BITS

Multi-profile bits like the ones shown in the drawing at right let you rout different profiles with the same bit. This is possible because there are a number of cutters stacked on the same bit. Raising or lowering the bit presents a different combination of cutters to the workpiece.

Multi-profile bits are most often used for making decorative moldings, but some are available that combine one or more joint-cutting profiles. The bit shown on pages 116–117 is designed to cut both halves of a cope-and-stick joint commonly used for frame-and-panel construction.

Although these bits pack a lot of profile punch, they do take longer to set up. You'll find that you have to make a number of test cuts, adjusting the bit up or down until the desired profile is achieved. Most woodworkers prefer the almost instant setup that a single-profile bit offers.

Also, because these bits are capable of routing many profiles, they are very expensive: the manufacturer is basically charging you for a multiple bit set. But as there's only a single shank, some savings are realized versus buying the bits separately.

Portable Router Accessories

There are a number of accessories that you can buy to make your router more accurate and easier and safer to use. Even if you own a router table or you're considering building one, these accessories will come in handy for those tasks that you can't accomplish on the router table.

Edge guides

Most router manufacturers make an edge guide for their routers that allow you to make cuts a limited distance in from the edge — typically 6" to 10" (at left in top photo). They're most useful for routing grooves, dadoes, and flutes. Some edge guides come with the tool; others can be purchased as an accessory. They range in quality and cost from a metal bracket that slides on a pair of rods that slip into the router base to elaborate extrusions that connect solidly to the base. Quality edge guides will allow for both rough and fine positioning. Keep in mind that you can increase the stability of most of these by attaching a long "outrigger" to the edge guide itself.

Router pads

A router pad is basically an open-weave foam cushion (middle photo). The open weave allows dust to pass through and will "grip" the workpiece to prevent it from sliding about. These pads are particularly useful when routing smaller parts, like the one shown in the photo. Router pads are virtually identical to the shelf padding used in recreational vehicles to keep items from shifting while on the road. It's a good idea to occasionally rinse the pad off with clean water and allow it to dry. This will keep the surface dust-free so it can provide a better grip.

Low-clearance clamps

A low-clearance or low-profile clamp is basically a straightedge with a built-in clamp that won't get in the way of your router — particularly the handles (bottom photo). If you've ever clamped a strip of wood to a workpiece and then run into the clamps with your router, you'll appreciate these. They're commonly available in 24", 36", and 50" lengths.

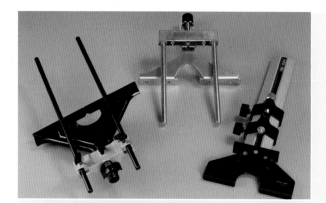

Dust pick-ups

Many woodworkers are first surprised and then alarmed at the quantity of chips and sawdust a router can produce, even when routing a single edge. Router manufacturers are quite aware of this problem — especially the health issues involved — and have made great strides in designing dust pick-ups. These vary from a simple plastic shroud to an elaborate replacement base plate with built-in collection (top photo). If you're buying a new router, check to see whether the manufacturer offers this valuable accessory. Even if you're not, check to see whether one is available for your current router: Your lungs will appreciate it.

Bushing sets

A bushing or template bushing set is a set of metal guides that fit in the bit opening of your router's base plate (middle photo). A metal collar screws onto the threads on top of each bushing to lock it in place. The bushings come in different diameters to let you vary the offset between the bit (typically a straight bit) and the template or guide it follows. Specialty jigs like sign-making jigs (see pages 84–85) and dovetail jigs (see pages 72–75) typically use a guide bushing with their jigs to guide the router bit.

INLAY SETS

If you're interested in adding inlays to your woodworking projects, consider buying an inlay set. This is basically a modified guide bushing set (see the photo at right). What makes this bushing special is the removable metal collar that slips over the business end of the bushing. This lets you use the same template to rout both the inlay and the inlay recess, guaranteeing a perfect fit. For more on how to use an inlay set, see pages 64–65.

Router Tables

If you've never mounted your router in a table, you're only utilizing half of its capabilities — maybe even less. Mounting a router in a table effectively turns in into a mini-shaper. You can accurately cut joints, work safely with small parts, and add a level of precision to your router work that may not have seemed possible. There's quite a variety of router tables on the market these days, everything from bench-top tables and stationary models to shop-made versions.

Bench-top

For woodworkers with limited space, a bench-top router just makes a lot of sense (top photo). Simply clamp the table to your workbench and you're ready to go. When shopping for a bench-top model, look for heavy castings to help dampen vibration, and a fence that allows for both rough and fine positioning. A dust chute is essential, as well as easy router mounting and removal.

Stationary router tables

If you have the shop space, we recommend a stationary router table. The mass of a larger table not only helps dampen vibration, but it also puts the work at the correct height and saves you the hassle of setting up a bench-top unit. You'll be surprised how quickly a stationary router table will become one of your most-used tools. You'll find router tables available with both open bases (photo at right) and closed bases (photos on the opposite page).

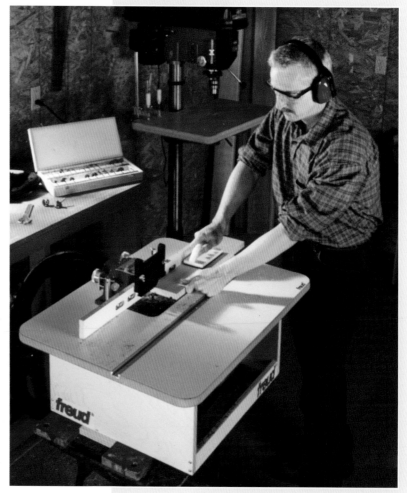

A closed-base system makes it easier to control and collect dust. The only disadvantage to a closed base is that it traps the heat generated by the router inside the cabinet. Well-designed router table cabinets will provide for some form of ventilation. If you use your router table a lot, consider installing a small muffin fan in the side of the cabinet. Add a vent opening in the opposite side to allow the fan to draw in fresh air and keep the router cool.

ROUTER TABLE OPTIONS

Most of the commercially available router tables have a number of optional add-ons you can purchase to make your router table more useful. Two of the most popular changes are making the table mobile and adding storage space.

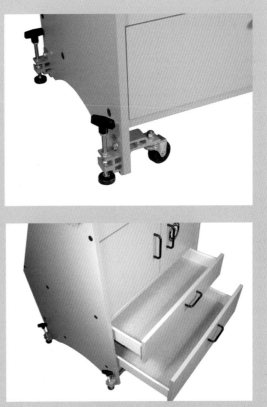

The mobile router table. Wheels for router tables can be as simple as locking castors, or as complex as the leveling system shown at top right made by Bench Dog (www.benchdog.com). This system combines swivel casters with a leveling system that allows you to move the router table with ease and then level it wherever it ends up. The leveling system consists of a knob on a threaded rod that terminates with a pad on the bottom. Just turn the knobs until the table is level, and then lock the levelers in place by tightening the lock nut that's captured in each extrusion. Each leveler is capable of lifting the table 1½".

Adding storage. Another popular option for a router table is adding drawers for additional storage (see the bottom photo at right). Here again, drawers can be simple slide-out units that rest on wood cleats or they can be drawers that attach to full-extension metal slides. Alternatively, you can add storage space under any table by attaching a pair of cleats to the sides or rails and adding a shelf; see the shop-made router table on pages 149–155 for more on this.

Shop-Made Router Tables

Although there are plans you can purchase for a number of shop-made router tables on the market, one of our favorites is the *ShopNotes* router table. The original plans for this table were published in *ShopNotes* magazine, Issue #1. It features a fully adjustable fence, bit storage, and replaceable insert. The router table can be made with either an open (top photo) or closed base (middle photo). The closed base does a great job of silencing the annoying whine a router makes. Plans are still available from *ShopNotes* project supplies at www.WoodsmithStore.com.

We've also included our own version of a shop-made router table on pages 149–155 (bottom photo). This table features a heavy top with a drop-in router plate. Step-by-step directions for making a fully adjustable fence to go along with the table can be found on pages 156–161.

When making your own router table, make sure to use materials that are dense to help dampen vibration. Medium-density fiberboard (MDF) is an excellent choice not only for the top because its super-flat surface accepts plastic laminates well, but also for the base, since the heavier it is, the better it will be able to reduce vibration. Particleboard can also be used, as it's flat and heavy, but it doesn't take fasteners as well as MDF.

If you're making an open-style base, consider using a dense hardwood such as the oak we used for our shop-made table. It costs more than softwood but will hold up better over time. Finally, whichever style you decide to build, take the time to apply a couple coats of clear finish to seal the wood against moisture, dirt, and grime.

Router Table Accessories

Router table fences

On a table saw the fence determines how usable and accurate the tool is. A good rip fence will slip easily into position and lock in solid. This is exactly what you want in a router fence. Additionally, a router fence should offer independently adjustable faces that open and close to surround a bit.

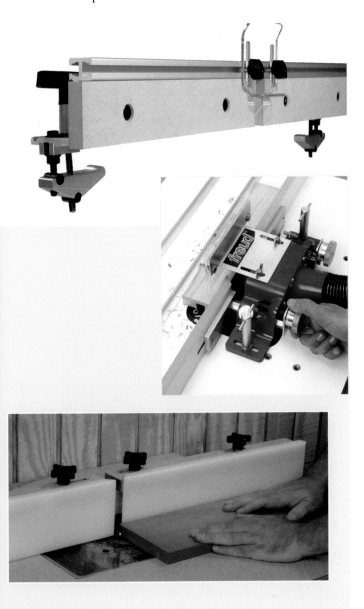

There are several manufactured fences available, and they vary in quality and features. The first thing to look at is the clamping mechanisms — that is, the clamps that secure the fence to the table. These should be accessible and have comfortable knobs, as you'll adjust them a lot. You'll find clamp knobs located on the top or bottom of the fence. Most woodworkers prefer clamp knobs on top because this gives better access. Whichever type you choose, just make sure that the clamps lock the fence securely in place. This is particularly a concern with a router table top that's covered with a slick surface like plastic laminate or melamine. Fences tend to slip a bit on these, so the locking mechanism must be able to exert sufficient pressure to prevent slippage.

The next feature to look at is the faces and how they adjust. The faces should be covered with laminate or another surface that will hold up well, since you'll be constantly pressing wood against them. The faces should slide back and forth on the body with precision. There should be some type of indexing system that keeps the faces aligned. And the faces should be able to slide completely closed. Because you'll be routinely adjusting the faces open and closed, they should be secured with readily accessible knobs — not screws. You don't want to have to pull out a screwdriver every time you want to adjust a fence face. Some fences, like the Freud fence shown in the photo at left, provide independently adjustable fence sections. This means you can move the fence section forward and backward by adjusting a knob. This is particularly useful if you want to joint on the router table, see page 126 for more on this. Finally, a quality fence system will have a bit guard and also offer some type of dust port to whisk away sawdust and chips. Deluxe fences also provide slots for mounting hold-downs, and stops.

You can make your own fence for a store-bought router table or for a table you've built yourself. For step-by-step construction details on a nifty fence that's easy to position, offers adjustable faces, and is rock-solid, see pages 156–161.

Router plates

If you're planning to buy a router table top, you'll find that it either comes with a plate or you can purchase one to fit in the pre-cut opening. Pre-made plates come either drilled for certain routers or as blanks, where you drill the mounting holes and bit openings yourself. Materials for plates are phenolic, acrylic, and metal. Phenolic and acrylic plates work well, but if not fully supported will bow over time — this is particularly true when a large router is suspended. Any router 3-hp or larger is best attached to a metal plate. The top left plate in the top photo comes pre-drilled as sort of a universal plate to handle most routers. Additional features to look for in a pre-made plate are interchangeable ring inserts that come in varying sizes; these let you alter the size of the bit opening. Many plates also offer a hole for a starting pin that's included with a plate.

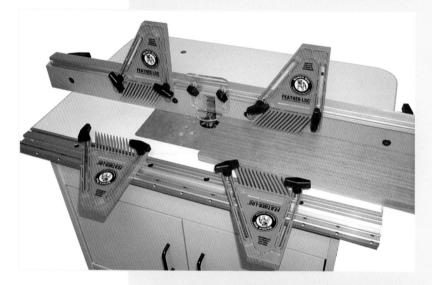

Hold-downs

Hold-downs are plastic feather-boards that mount either to slots in the fence or to the miter gauge, or can be clamped to either the fence or the table (middle photo). These are indispensable safety aids to make sure a workpiece is firmly pressed against the fence and incapable of kicking back. The angled fingers prevent kickback by allowing a workpiece to travel only forward — that is, as long as the featherboard is installed properly. It should be adjusted so the fingers will bend slightly as the workpiece passes by.

Stops

Another nice accessory for the router table fence is a sliding stop block (bottom photo). As with hold-downs, these are typically designed to slide in a slot in the fence and are usually sold to work in a specific fence system.

Bit guards

Bit guards attach to a fence to keep fingers away from spinning bits (top photo). They should be fully adjustable and also removable if necessary. In addition to sliding up and down, the guard shown here, manufactured by Freud, also adjusts in and out — a feature you won't find in many guards. To offer a clear view of the bit, a guard should always be made of transparent plastic. As with any other shop safety feature, a bit guard can't do its job if it isn't used.

Dust chutes

Most manufactured router table fences offer some type of chute for dust control. The chute attaches to the back of the fence over the bit opening or directly to the table to collect dust (middle photo). Chute sizes vary from one manufacturer to another, but adapters are available to allow you to hook it up to your shop vacuum or dust collection system. Chutes can be found with simple openings or with extended collars so you can slip on flexible tubing.

Plunge router handles

Since so many woodworkers who purchase plunge routers mount them in a router table, most plunge router manufacturers have begun to supply a long or extended-height adjustment handle with the routers. These handles thread onto the height-adjustment rod and make it easy to vary the depth of cut when the router is mounted upside down on a table. The only disadvantage to most of these is that it often takes a whole lot of twisting to adjust a bit to the desired depth of cut. That's why handles with cranks, like the one shown in the bottom photo, manufactured by Woodhaven (www.woodhaven.com), make adjustments fast and easy.

Router lifts

It's no surprise that someone eventually came up with a router lift. Woodworkers have grumbled for years about having to get down on their knees to change or adjust a bit in a router mounted in a table. Router lifts take away the drudgery of this task, letting you adjust the bit height from above via a removable crank handle (top photo). Many lifts are designed for specific routers and are best used if you have two routers: one dedicated to a router table and another for portable use. That's because a lift attaches to a router, making it awkward to use as a portable. Yes, you can remove the lift every time, but this can be both time-consuming and frustrating. Router lifts vary considerably in pricing and ease of use — consider checking out the online woodworking forums before buying one.

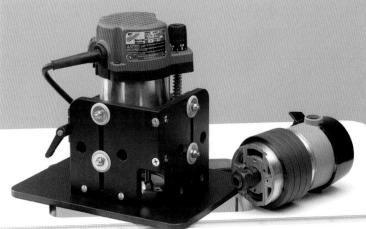

Positioning jigs

Positioning jigs like the Incra jig (www.incra.com) shown in the photo at right are designed to accurately position a router table fence in exacting increments. This is extremely useful when cutting intricate joinery like both joints and dovetails, where even a fraction of an inch of error can be the difference between the joint fitting or not fitting together. The Incra jig comes with interchangeable templates that make it easy to cut a variety of joinery, including box joints and both half-blind and through dovetails.

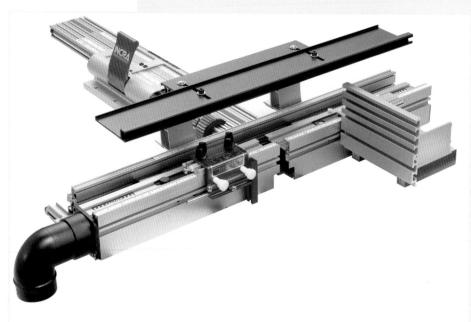

ROUTER SLEDS

A fairly recent development, router sleds are becoming a popular router table accessory because they can add precision to your work while also making cuts easier and safer to make. Router sleds are designed to hold a workpiece secure for a cut without putting your hands in jeopardy. They typically consist of a base unit (the sled), which has a fence and one or more clamping devices attached to it. Handles or knobs attached to it offer convenient handholds for moving the sled. Sleds can be guided by either a fence or the miter gauge track.

Router sleds excel at holding frame parts for cutting cope-and-stick joints (see pages 116–117 for more on this joint). They're also handy for cutting tenons and lap joints, and any operation where you'd normally use a miter gauge to push the workpiece past the spinning bit.

Miter gauge–guided sleds. If your router table has a miter gauge slot in it, you'll find that the miter gauge version of the router sled is easy to set up and use. A miter gauge bar is attached beneath the sled to fit into the slot in your table (top photo). The miter gauge bars on many sleds are adjustable so you can tweak them to remove any side-to-side play.

Fence-guided sleds. The other version of the router sled is the style shown in the bottom photo. It slides along the router table fence instead of the tracking in the miter gauge slot. The advantage to this type is that you can position it for use anywhere along the width of the table. You don't have to worry about where your miter gauge slot is with respect to the bit. On the downside, this type of sled takes more time to set up versus the miter gauge slot variety.

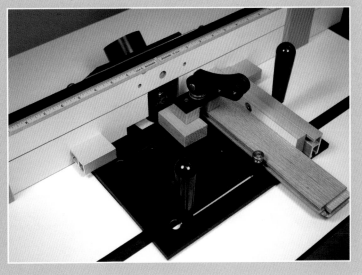

Router Jigs

Circle jigs

A circle jig allows you to cut a perfect circle in varying diameters. These jigs range from simple to complex. A simple circle jig is basically an auxiliary base plate that's long and tapered and attaches to your router. A pivot pin (usually just a nail or a screw) is driven into the workpiece to serve as a pivot. More deluxe versions provide a pivot plate that attaches to your workpiece without marring its surface (top photo). This connects to an arm that lets you accurately position the router. (See pages 136–137 for a shop-made version of this jig.)

Hinge-mortising jigs

Hinge-mortising jigs, like the one shown in the middle photo at right, let you accurately cut and set hinges in minutes. Most hinge-mortising jigs rout recesses for hinges ranging from 1" to 5" in length. Some are adjustable; others are designed solely for cutting mortises for door hinges. For more on mortising hinges, see page 80.

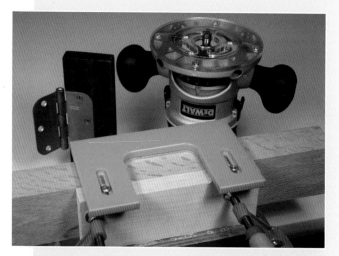

Dovetail jigs

The dovetail jig is one of the most popular accessories for a portable router because it allows even a beginning woodworker to cut precise, perfect-fitting dovetails. Dovetail jigs vary considerably in cost and features. Some can cut only half-blind dovetails. Others can cut half-blind and full dovetails as well as box joints and a variety of other joints. Regardless of the joint-cutting ability, any dovetail jig should offer built-in clamps that are easy to use and that solidly secure a workpiece. Simple jigs use single-piece templates, while more advanced jigs (like the Akeda DC-16V shown in the bottom photo) provide individual pieces so that you can vary pin and tail spacing. For more on dovetails, see pages 72–75.

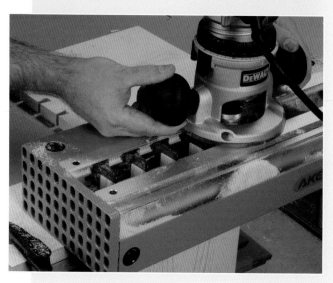

Letter and sign carving

Another popular specialty jig lets you rout your own signs. The jig shown in the photo at left, made by Craftsman, uses a set of plastic letter templates and a guide bushing to accurately craft signs. The letter templates slip into channels in the guide rods, and this entire assembly is then clamped to your workpiece. Letters can be routed with a straight bit or core-box bit, and additional templates with different fonts are available. For more on sign-making, see pages 83–85.

Box-joint jig

The box-joint jig shown in the middle photo is made by Woodsmith (www.WoodsmithStore.com). Although shown on the table saw here, the jig also attaches to your router table miter gauge and is fully adjustable, so you can vary pin spacing from $1/4$" to $13/16$". To prevent your workpiece from chipping out as the bit exits the workpiece, there are plastic backing strips that slip into a recess in the back of the jig. These can be replaced as needed.

HORIZONTAL MORTISER

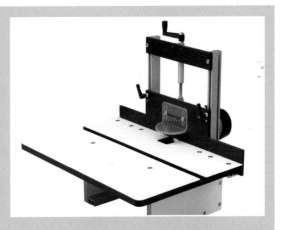

If you think about it, mounting a router horizontally to a table makes a lot of sense. It's a whole lot easier to cut mortises this way, as you can slide the workpiece evenly into the rotating bit instead of dropping it down from above. That's because gravity is working for you with the router mounted horizontally, instead of against you when it's vertical. With the workpiece lying flat on the table, there's no chance of it wiggling as it's pushed into the bit. But these jigs aren't just for mortising. Odds are that you'll find yourself using yours for many other cuts. For instance, making raised panels with a vertical panel-raising bit is a natural here, as now the workpiece is lying flat on the table — and there's much less bit exposed than you'd have with a conventional panel-raising bit. The jig shown here is manufactured by Woodhaven (www.woodhaven.com).

3 Handheld Router Techniques

The day many woodworkers purchase their first router is the day many become better woodworkers. That's because a router adds a whole new dimension to woodworking. Sure, you can now profile and edge, and that's nice. But how about making an amazing array of joints that slip together with precision? Grooves and dadoes, rabbets, mortise-and-tenons — even dovetails are possible with the addition of this simple tool. Did you know that you can create beautiful inlays with a portable router? How about making signs?

All it takes besides a router to do all this is a little knowledge and some simple guides. And that's what this chapter is all about. We'll take you step-by-step through the how-to of a handheld router: everything from routing direction and feed rate to preventing chip-out. Then we'll move on to joinery and advanced techniques like routing mortises for hinges and duplicating parts with ease.

Beginning woodworkers will wonder how they lived without a router, and experienced craftsmen will learn to teach their router some new tricks.

The number of things you can do with a handheld router is amazing. Want to build a simple bookcase using grooves and dadoes? Craft a chest of drawers held together with dovetail joints? Make signs, or inlay delicate pattern into wood? It's all possible with this single tool.

Routing Direction

For all its versatility, the router is a surprisingly simple tool to operate. There are only a couple of rules to keep in mind — most importantly, routing direction and proper grip.

they're first turned on and have a tendency to twist or kick. That doesn't mean you want a white-knuckle grip. On the contrary, you're looking for a grip similar to how you should hold the steering wheel of a car: firm, but relaxed. Too loose and the router can get away from you; too tight and you'll find it's tougher to control. Rigid muscles tend to create jerky movements — and these will transfer to your cuts.

Feed direction

The number one router rule concerns the feed direction — that is, how you move the router with respect to the workpiece. Since the router bit always rotates in the same direction (clockwise if you look at it from above), it's important to move the router so the bit will enter the wood correctly and pull it into the workpiece. When routing an outside edge, move the router counterclockwise; for an inside edge, move it clockwise (see the drawing above). If you move the router in the wrong direction (referred to as backrouting), you'll know immediately, as the router bit will tend to bounce off the workpiece and "run" along its edge. Occasionally, backrouting has its uses; see page 56.

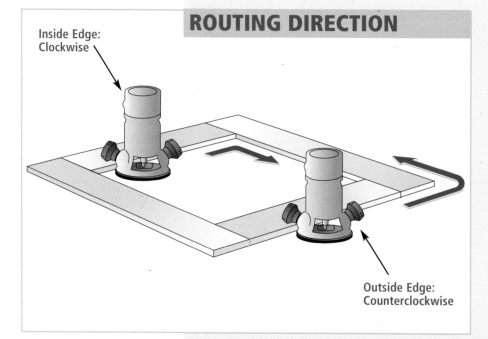

ROUTING DIRECTION

Inside Edge: Clockwise

Outside Edge: Counterclockwise

Proper grip

Although some routers, such as laminate trimmers, are designed for one-handed use, you should always grip a fixed-base or plunge router firmly by both handles when routing. This is particularly important with routers with $1^1/_2$-horsepower or larger motors. These larger routers can be quite "torquey" when

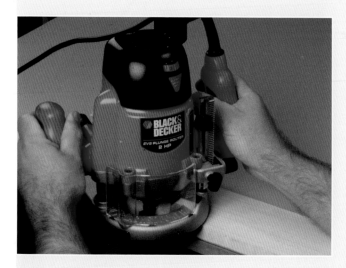

Speed and Feed Rate

The speed at which the bit rotates and the rate at which you feed the bit into a workpiece will determine the quality of the cut — as long as the bit is sharp. A dull bit will cause a poor cut. Period. For information on sharpening router bits, see pages 174–175.

Router speed

When routers first hit the market decades ago, they came in only a single-speed version, typically around 24,000 rpm. With basically no option for changing speed, you had to learn how to vary the feed rate (see below) for the best cut. Single-speed routers also are limited in the size of the bit they can handle safely. As a general rule of thumb, you want to decrease speed as bit diameter increases (see the chart below left). That's because the actual rim speed — that is, the speed at the outermost cutting edge of the bit — is very fast on large bits because of their greater diameters. Single-speed routers can be made variable with the use of a speed control, but these tend to decrease the life of the router's motor, as it causes them to run at speeds they were never designed for. Today's variable-speed routers make varying speed as simple as turning a knob (middle photo).

Feed rate

Even if you select the perfect bit speed for your router, you'll get a poor cut if you use the incorrect feed rate. Unfortunately, there is no firm rule for feed rate — you really have to learn this by trial and error (preferably on scrap wood). When you find the correct combination of bit speed and feed rate, the bit will create fine shavings, not dust, and there will be no burning or chatter. Burning (as shown in the top left photo) is usually caused by too slow a feed rate. Chatter, which looks like tiny scallops on the edge of the cut, is caused by a rate that's too fast. A final sign of feed rate is the sound of the router. Over time, you'll eventually learn to recognize the drop in tone that indicates you're feeding too fast and are trying to remove too much wood.

ROUTER SPEEDS

Material	Bit Diameter	Maximum Speed
Wood	Up to 1"	20,000 – 24,000 rpm
	1¼" – 2"	18,000 rpm
	2¼" – 2½"	16,000 rpm
	3" – 3½"	8,000 – 14,000 rpm
Plastics	Up to 1"	13,000 – 16,000 rpm
	1¼" – 2"	10,000 – 13,000 rpm
Aluminum	Up to 1"	12,000 – 16,000 rpm
	1¼" – 2"	8,000 – 12,000 rpm

Depth of Cut

How you adjust bit height, or depth of cut, depends on the type of router (fixed-base or plunge) and the mechanism used by the manufacturer.

Fixed-base router

The most common height-adjustment mechanism for fixed-base routers is the pin-and-groove or collar-and-groove, as shown in the top photo. With this type of system, once the bit is installed, you release the locking mechanism that pinches the split base on the motor unit. This is either a knob that's turned, or a toggle that's flipped. Then it's simply a matter of rotating the motor unit up or down to achieve the desired depth of cut. Most routers have an adjustable plastic collar that fits on top of the motor base and is used for rough positioning. To use one of these, lower the bit until it rests on the surface of the workpiece. Then rotate the friction-tight adjustment collar until it reads "zero." Now when you rotate the motor unit, the adjustment collar will provide a rough readout of bit depth. Remember: This should be used only for rough positioning; always make a test cut in a scrap of wood for final adjustment.

Plunge router

The depth of cut on plunge routers can be adjusted two ways. The quick way is to release the locking lever and plunge the router down until the bit protrudes out from the base the desired depth, then lock it in place with the lever (middle photo); but it's tough to hit the exact height. A more precise way is to use a micro-adjust knob threaded onto the stop rod; see page 34 for more on these.

Depth stops

Because of the difficulty of adjusting bit height on a plunge router, manufacturers have added depth stops, which make it easy to fine-tune the bit's position. A depth stop prevents the router from plunging further when the stop rod hits the router base, or more commonly, a pivoting stop turret. Stop turrets typically have three adjustable stops that can be rotated to position any of the three under the depth stop rod (bottom photo). This lets you rout a mortise in, say, three steps without turning off the router to adjust the depth of cut. You just return the router to its up position, pivot the turret, and plunge for the next deeper pass. As with any fixed-base router, the depth indicator on a plunge router is best used only for rough positioning.

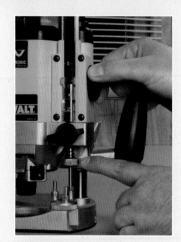

HEIGHT-ADJUSTMENT JIG

Here's a simple jig that will make adjusting bit height simple and accurate. This jig can be used on portable routers and routers mounted in a table.

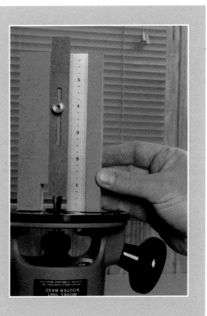

Construction. The height-adjustment jig consists of two parts, a body and a slide, and uses a 6" metal rule for measurements. The rule is held in place by a pair of round magnets set into the body. To make the body, cut a piece of MDF (medium-density fiberboard) to a width of 3¼" and a length of 6". Then rout a pair of grooves as shown in the Top View. The innermost groove accepts the slide, and the groove closest to the edge holds the metal rule in place. The far edge of the groove for the slide is 2" from the edge and is ⅛" deep and ¾" wide. The groove for the rule is ½" in from the edge and is cut to match the width and thickness of the metal rule.

Next, cut a 1"-wide by 1"-tall notch in the bottom of the body 1¼" in from the edge. This notch allows you to position the jig directly over a bit. Finally, drill stopped holes for two magnets in the metal rule groove and epoxy them in place (we used ½" round magnets). To make the slide, cut a piece of ⅛" hardboard ¾" wide and 6" long. Then rout a 2¼", ⅛"-wide slot centered on the slide, 2" up from the bottom. Place the slide in the groove in the body and make a mark at the top of the slot. Drill a hole through the body here, and thread a screw through the body from behind. Secure the slide with a washer and knurled knob as shown.

In use. To use the jig, place the metal rule in its groove so it's flush with the bottom (the magnets will hold it in place). Then loosen the knurled knob and adjust the slide for the desired depth of cut — the bottom of the slide serves as the indicator. Position the jig over the bit and simply raise the bit until it contacts the slide, for quick and accurate positioning.

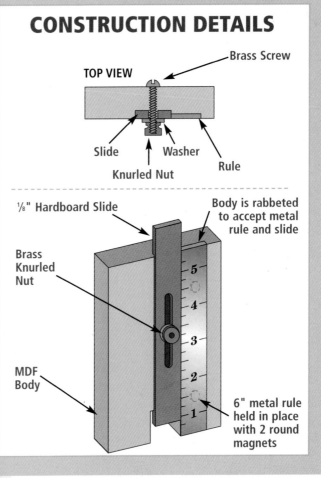

CONSTRUCTION DETAILS

TOP VIEW

Brass Screw

Slide

Knurled Nut

Washer

Rule

⅛" Hardboard Slide

Brass Knurled Nut

MDF Body

Body is rabbeted to accept metal rule and slide

6" metal rule held in place with 2 round magnets

Stabilizing a Cut

For a router to make an accurate cut, the router bit needs to be perpendicular to the face of the workpiece. The router base can handle this task on most cuts, especially when the full base rides on the workpiece (such as when routing a groove or dado). However, on edge cuts, where one-half of the base extends unsupported past the workpiece, the router can tip, ruining the cut. There are a couple of ways to prevent this.

Use a fence
You can stabilize a cut when routing near an edge by using a fence attachment for the router (top photo). This will help ensure that the router base lies flat on the workpiece and perfectly parallel to the edge.

Add an outrigger
For routing tasks where the router base does not completely rest on the workpiece, such as when profiling an edge, it's best to have extra support to keep the router from tipping toward the unsupported side. One way to provide this support is to lay a scrap of wood the same thickness as the workpiece an inch or two away from the edge as a sort of outrigger so the unsupported section can ride on it (middle photo). This will work only with a bit whose depth is set to less than the thickness of the workpiece.

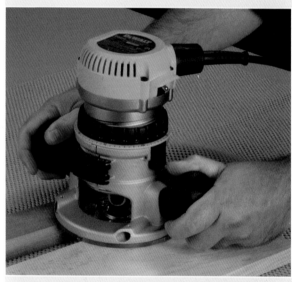

Add block to base
Another way to add support is to temporarily fasten a scrap-wood "outrigger" with double-sided tape under the unsupported section of the router base so it will move along with the cut (bottom photo). This works well on long cuts, where using a long piece of scrap as described above wouldn't be feasible. It's imperative that the scrap outrigger match the thickness of the workpiece. The surface it rides on must also be level and smooth, or you'll get an irregular cut.

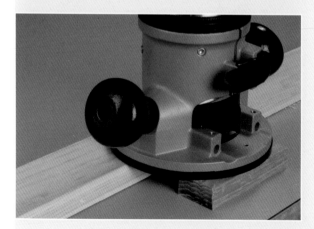

MULTIPLE PASSES

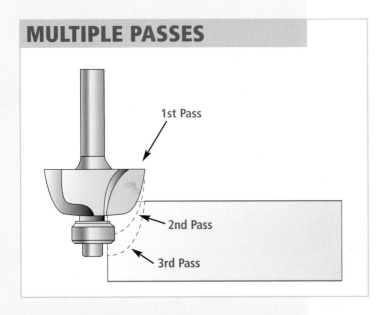

1st Pass

2nd Pass

3rd Pass

Take multiple passes

Probably the most common mistake among beginning woodworkers (and even some seasoned veterans) is to try to make a router cut in a single pass. Although some heavy-duty routers are capable of this, there are a number of reasons why taking a series of lighter, multiple passes is better (see drawing at left). First, a lighter cut tends to chip-out less. Second, it's easier on the bit and router. Third, the cut is easier to control and will end up more precise and smoother, with less burning. A good general rule of thumb is to take three equal cuts to reach a full profile. For an extra-smooth finish, consider taking three lighter cuts and a final, super-light cut.

WORKING WITH PLASTIC

Plastics have become increasingly popular in the woodshop. Unlike wood, which swells and shrinks as the humidity changes, plastic is dimensionally stable. This makes it perfect for making jigs and fixtures for the shop, where precision is paramount. The different types of plastic offer additional benefits. Clear plastics like acrylic are perfect for router plates and oversized base plates because they let you see what you're routing (see page 133 for an example of this). Other plastics like UHMW (ultra-high molecular weight) offer hard surfaces that are slick. These are excellent for use as a fence face where workpieces are constantly being pressed along the surface (see the router table fence on page 156 for an example of UHMW in action).

Routing plastic. Most plastics such as Lexan, Plexiglas, and acrylic can be routed quite satisfactorily. If you have a variable-speed router, slow the speed down to around 13,000 rpm for most bits. Larger bits should be used around 10,000 rpm. The reason for slowing down the router is that high speeds tend to actually melt the plastic instead of cutting it. As usual, you're better off taking multiple, light passes than a single heavy pass. Also, feed rate should be slightly faster, since any hesitation and the resulting friction of bit against plastic will cause melting.

Tear-out and Chip-out

Tear-out and chip-out are the two most common problems you'll face when routing (see the photos at right). Both problems are caused by the bit exiting the edge of the workpiece. Unsupported wood fibers can be torn out of the edge, or larger pieces or chips can splinter off. Although chip-out is the more severe of the two, the terms are often used interchangeably.

Here's what happens: As a router bit enters the edge of a workpiece, the wood fibers behind the cutting edge of the bit are backed up or supported by the inner wood fibers of the workpiece. But when the bit exits the workpiece, there is no wood to back up the fibers at the edge. So when the bit pops out of the edge, the unsupported wood fibers will either tear-out or chip-out, leaving a jagged cut.

There are a number of ways to prevent either problem. By far the simplest method is to take light passes and shallow cuts. Although we probably sound like a broken record by now about multiple passes, this technique can help prevent many problems, including chip-out. If you take a shallow first cut, let's say with a rabbeting bit, you'll remove the wood fibers that are most prone to chip-out (see the drawing at right). Then you can take one or two more passes to finish the cut. Sure, this takes longer, but the effort will pay off with clean cuts, more finished-looking projects, and less wasted wood from having to remake parts that have chipped-out.

The edge of a workpiece can tear-out or chip-out, but it's the corners that you really have to worry about: Even light passes can't help the unsupported wood fibers at the end of a workpiece. There are a number of tricks to get around this common problem, as explained in the sidebar on the opposite page.

CHIP-OUT AND ITS SOLUTION

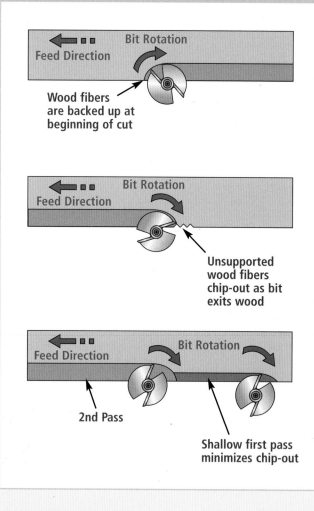

Feed Direction · Bit Rotation

Wood fibers are backed up at beginning of cut

Feed Direction · Bit Rotation

Unsupported wood fibers chip-out as bit exits wood

Feed Direction · Bit Rotation

2nd Pass

Shallow first pass minimizes chip-out

PREVENTING TEAR-OUT AND CHIP-OUT

Do ends first. One method to prevent chip-out doesn't actually prevent it, it just removes it after it has occurred. Although this sounds confusing, it's all about routing sequence. This method works only if you're routing the ends and at least one side of a workpiece. The secret is to rout the ends first, see the photo at right. This way, any chip-out that does occur will be removed when you rout the sides. You'll still need to take care to minimize the chip-out by taking light cuts. Obviously, if you chip-out a big chunk of wood, no amount of routing the side edges will be able to hide it.

Use support piece. Another method for preventing chip-out also doesn't prevent it. It allows it, except this time the chip-out occurs on a scrap of wood clamped to your workpiece (see the middle photo at right). The scrap piece will fully support the wood fibers as the bit leaves the workpiece and enters the scrap. No chip-out will occur here — only at the end of the scrap piece, where it doesn't matter.

Go both directions. The final method to prevent a corner from chipping-out is to backrout just the first inch or two of the edge, as shown in the bottom photo. Then the remainder of the edge can be routed using standard feed direction (see page 56 for more on backrouting). Here again, you should do this only on a workpiece that's clamped securely to a work surface, and make sure to take several light cuts.

Backrouting

Backrouting is a technique that can be used to help prevent chip-out. Basically, the router is moved opposite the normal direction so the cutting edge of the bit can't lift out slivers of wood, commonly called chip-out or tear-out (top drawing). Backrouting is a dangerous technique and should be attempted only after you feel comfortable with your router. That's because when backrouting, the bit won't pull itself into the wood as it normally does, and the router will tend to skip or bounce along the edge. If you decide to try this, take light cuts and keep a firm grip on the router. DO NOT backrout small pieces on a table-mounted router — the router bit can grab the workpiece and pull it and your fingers into the spinning bit.

Clamp the workpiece
The main rule for backrouting with a portable router is to securely clamp the workpiece to your bench or work surface (middle photo). If you don't, and you've got a good grip on the router and it's of sufficient horsepower, it could easily pick the workpiece up and throw it across the room in an instant. Use two clamps at minimum and tighten them forcefully. Do not backrout using a portable router with a work-piece resting on a router pad: The pad will not grip the workpiece, and you'll surely have an accident.

Backrouting technique
Because a router bit will skip along the edge of the workpiece when backrouting, a firm grip on the router is essential. Feed rate is slower than normal, as you don't want to try to remove a lot of wood. If, say, you're routing a rabbet (bottom photo), all you want to do is take a light cut to remove wood at the very edge of the workpiece, where it tends to chip-out. Once this is done, go back and take another pass in the normal feed direction. Continue taking passes in the normal direction until the profile is complete.

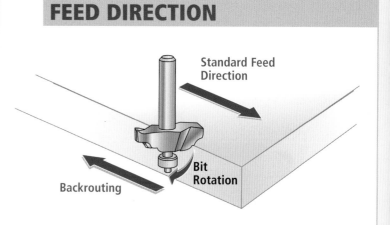

FEED DIRECTION

Standard Feed Direction

Backrouting

Bit Rotation

Router Safety

Working safely with a router is easy as long as you protect your eyes, ears, and lungs and follow a few simple rules about securing the workpiece.

Protect yourself

For a small tool, the router can produce an impressive amount of dust and chips. And quite often you'll have your face very near the router as you watch the bit make its cut. That's why you should always wear eye protection when using a router. The best type of eye protection is the wrap-around style shown in the top photo at left, as this prevents anything from coming in through the sides. Because the small electric motors on most routers tend to whine considerably, it's also a good idea to don some form of ear protection: ear plugs, or better yet, a set of muffs, to dampen sound. Additionally, if your router doesn't have some form of dust collection, you should protect your lungs by wearing a dust mask or respirator.

Secure the workpiece

One of the most common accidents that can happen when routing is workpiece movement. The bit can hang up in the workpiece and throw it or cause it to shift and ruin the cut. Prevent this by firmly clamping the workpiece to a work surface. When possible, always secure the workpiece with two clamps (middle photo). Yes, you'll have to move the clamps one at a time if you're routing along the entire length of the board (as they're in the path of the router), but you'll be able to make the cut safely.

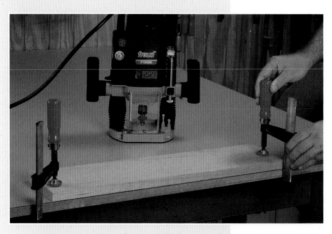

Make stable cuts

Another routing accident can occur when a cut is attempted that isn't stable, such as routing along the thin edge of a workpiece. The thin edge doesn't offer a wide enough base for the router, so the tool will wobble during the cut, an unsafe condition. When faced with a cut like this, add some auxiliary support by clamping the workpiece to a wider piece of scrap as shown in the bottom photo. This will create a solid foundation for a safe cut.

Freehand Routing

Freehand routing is a technique not often used by most woodworkers. That's because, since there are no guides to follow, the bit is totally controlled by the user. Unless the hand and arm movements directing the router are smooth, the bit will rout an uneven path. That's why wood selection is important if you're planning to try freehand routing. Woods with clearly defined growth rings (indicating seasonal growth of early and late wood) are difficult to rout smoothly freehand because the early wood and late wood are of different densities. This means the bit will plow though the early wood easily and then slow down at the late wood, producing a ragged, jerky cut. Stick with fine-grained woods such as birch, maple, and poplar.

Basic technique

Freehand routing is most often used for making signs or routing one-of-a-kind decorations (top photo). In order to do this, you'll need to choose an unpiloted bit (see pages 30–31). The straight bit and core-box bit are two popular choices. Since it's tough to replicate a free-form motion, rout with the bit set to the desired final depth. You can trace a design or letters on the workpiece or simply have at it. Either way, keep a firm grip on the router and make your movements as smooth as possible. A plunge router works best for freehand routing, as it's easiest to start and stop routing by plunging and releasing as needed.

Laminate trimmer

Some woodworkers prefer using a laminate trimmer for sign making; they find the single-handed grip more conducive to graceful movements (middle photo). The disadvantage: Extra care must be taken when starting and stopping cuts. Without plunging action, it's easy to burn wood if you hesitate or make a jagged cut when entering or exiting the workpiece.

Oversized base plate

Another common application of freehand routing is cleaning out waste. An example of this would be the shallow tray being routed in the bottom photo. Once the inside edges have been defined, the waste can be removed. In situations like these, an oversized base plate comes in handy to safely span from edge to edge. For step-by-step directions on how to make an oversized base plate, see pages 133–135.

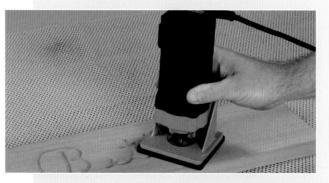

Piloted Cuts

Cuts made with piloted bits are by far the simplest to make: It's just a matter of letting the bearing on the bit guide the workpiece. As long as you use the correct feed direction (see page 48) and take light passes, there should little problem. The three most common piloted cuts are round-overs, chamfers, and decorative profiles.

Round-overs

Any round-over with a radius larger than $1/8$" should be made with multiple passes to prevent chip-out (top left photo). A $1/8$" round-over bit, commonly used to soften edges, is fine at full depth. When routing soft woods, consider using an edge guide as described on page 175 to prevent bearing tracks, which are indentations left in the edge of the wood, caused by pressing the bearing too hard against the edge. A variation of the round-over is the lipped round-over, where the bit is lowered to the point that the flat upper portion of the bit cuts into the edge and face of the workpiece, leaving a lip (see inset). Be careful with this final pass, as the wood fibers on the face of the workpiece are unsupported and will chip-out easily.

Chamfers

Unlike round-over bits, where you'll need to change bits for the different radii, a chamfer bit is capable of cutting any depth up to its maximum cut (middle photo). All you need do is lower the bit for the desired size. Multiple passes are again called for, and you'll need to be especially careful at the corners. That's because, unlike the gentle radius of a round-over, the sharp angle of the chamfer really tends to knock off chips at the corners.

Decorative profiles

The only challenge to working with a decorative profile bit, like a Roman ogee, for example, is not cutting the full profile in a single pass (bottom photo). Beginning woodworkers often lower the bit to expose the desired profile and start routing. This, of course, will cause several problems, including chip-out and burning. Take light cuts and sneak up on the final profile.

Guided Cuts

A guided cut is any cut made with a portable router that doesn't use a piloted bit. The most common guides used with a portable router are edge guides and clamp-on straightedges; they're used primarily to rout grooves and dadoes (top drawing at right). A dado is a U-shaped cross-grain cut on the face of a piece of wood that's sized to accept another part. The cousin of the dado is the groove, a U-shaped cut that's made with the grain instead of across it. A dado is cut across the width of a board, while a groove is cut along its length. Both of these joints are excellent ways to lock one part into another.

Although it may seem like nit-picking here, using the correct nomenclature to describe a cut as either a groove or a dado is important when communicating with other woodworkers. You wouldn't call a Ford a Chevy, would you? They're both cars, right? Just like a groove and a dado are both U-shaped cuts made in the face of a workpiece.

How far a groove or dado is in from the edge of a board will determine which guide you use to make the cut. For grooves and dadoes near the edge, an edge guide will work fine. When they're farther in from the edge than an edge guide can reach, the straightedge is the guide to use.

Mark router base for reference

Whenever you use a straightedge to guide a router through its cut, it's important to keep the same point of the router base in contact with the straightedge as you move it along its length. Why? Because most router bases aren't perfectly round. This means if you rotate the router as you move it along the straightedge, the router cut will not be perfectly parallel to the straightedge. Depending on the router base, this could be an insignificant variation, or large enough to cause problems. To prevent this, it's a good idea to make a visible reference mark on the base and keep this mark against the straightedge as you rout (see the bottom drawing).

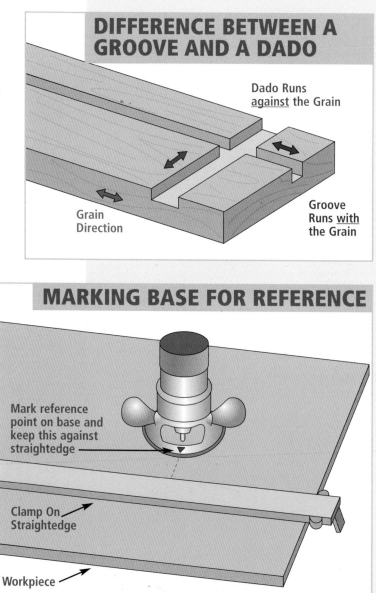

DIFFERENCE BETWEEN A GROOVE AND A DADO

Dado Runs <u>against</u> the Grain

Grain Direction

Groove Runs <u>with</u> the Grain

MARKING BASE FOR REFERENCE

Mark reference point on base and keep this against straightedge

Clamp On Straightedge

Workpiece

Using a Straightedge as a Guide

Want accurate cuts using a straightedge? The operative word is straight. Although this should be obvious, a lot of woodworkers will pick up any stick of lumber in the shop and use it. Your best bet is to rip

both edges of a scrap of plywood or MDF (medium-density fiberboard) to ensure they're parallel. If you do use a scrap of wood, first check it against a known flat surface such as the top of a table saw or the bed of a jointer. Alternatively, if you use your router to cut a lot of grooves and dadoes, consider making the straightedge shown on pages 130–132. This nifty jig makes it easy to rout grooves and dadoes precisely.

Position the straightedge

There are a number of ways to set up a straightedge to make a cut. The most accurate is to actually lay out the groove or dado on the workpiece and then adjust the fence to position the router bit over the marked cut. A simple way to do this is to position the router with the bit in place over the mark and slide the fence over until it butts up against the router. Then clamp one end of the straightedge and use a tape measure or rule to make sure it's parallel to the edge of the workpiece (top photo at left). Finally, reposition the router to make sure nothing has shifted, and clamp the other end.

Add support to the end

When you reach the end of a cut using a straightedge, two problems can occur. First, the bit can cause chip-out as it exits the workpiece. Second, the router can tip or tilt, since the leading edge is no longer resting on the workpiece. Both problems go away when you clamp a support block to the end of the workpiece (middle photo). The block prevents chip-out by supporting the wood fibers at the end of the cut and keeps the router from tipping by supporting the leading edge. Just make sure that the support block is the same thickness as the workpiece.

Make the cut

With the straightedge and support block in place you can make your cuts. As usual, it's best to take light, multiple passes until the desired depth of cut is reached. Keep the router's reference point (see opposite page) against the straightedge and press the router firmly against the straightedge as you move it along for the cut.

Using an Edge Guide

Edge guides make quick work of routing grooves and dadoes, because the guide attaches directly to the router instead of the workpiece, as with a straightedge.

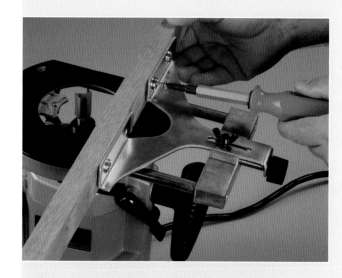

Add an auxiliary fence

Even the most deluxe edge guide can benefit from the addition of an auxiliary fence (top photo). That's because the fence portion of most edge guides is very short; this can cause problems at the beginning and end of a cut, where only one half of the edge guide's fence is contacting the workpiece. An auxiliary fence provides a longer fence to keep in contact with the workpiece and to prevent miscuts. Most edge guides have holes in the fence for attaching an auxiliary fence.

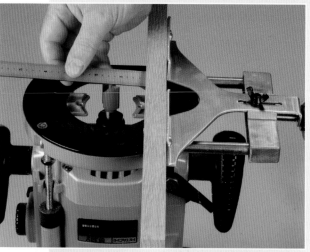

Set up the fence

To position the fence of the edge guide, use a metal rule or tape measure to set the bit-to-fence distance (middle photo). Better edge guides will have some form of micro-adjustment that will make it easy to fine-tune the position. Once set, lock the fence in place by tightening the appropriate knob or knobs.

Make the cut

Now you can cut the groove or dado. First press the leading half of the long auxiliary fence against the edge of the workpiece and slowly move it along until the bit enters the wood (bottom photo). As you make the cut, press the full length of the auxiliary fence against the workpiece edge. Firm, even pressure is what you want here. Continue cutting until you reach the end of the workpiece. Then transfer pressure to the trailing half of the auxiliary fence as the bit exits the wood.

MAKING STOPPED CUTS

Many woodworking projects call for stopped cuts. These are cuts that stop a set distance from an edge. An example of this would be stopped rabbets on the back edges of a bookcase to accept the back of the bookcase. Stopping the rabbets means the edges of the back — typically plywood — will remain hidden by the sides and top and bottom of the case.

Lay out the ends of the cut. To make a stopped cut, start by laying out where you want the cut to stop on the workpiece (see the middle photo). Note that we used a white pencil here to make the mark highly visible on the dark hardwood.

Position the stop or stops. Next, clamp a scrap of wood to the workpiece to stop the router at the desired position. You'll need to offset the stop block away from the mark to match the distance from the router bit to the edge of the router base. The easiest way to do this is to simply position the router (with the bit inserted) on the workpiece so the bit is over the marked line. Use a try square to position the block so it's perpendicular to the edge of the workpiece, as shown in the bottom photo.

Make the cut. To make the stopped cut, set the router on the workpiece with the bit away from the edge and the router base touching the stop. Then turn on the router and gently ease the bit into the workpiece. As soon as it starts to cut, begin moving the router along the edge. If you hesitate at all, you'll get burning. Continue moving the router along the edge until you hit the opposite stop. When it hits the stop, immediately pull it away from the edge to prevent burning.

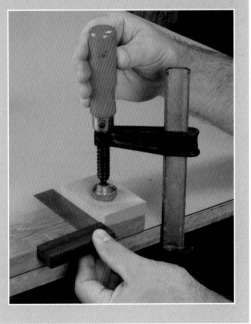

Inlay Systems

If you've ever wanted to add an inlay to a project but thought it was beyond your skill level, you'll enjoy working with an inlay system. Inlay systems are specialized guide bushings (see page 35) that allow anyone to make and set an inlay into a project with absolute precision (see the top photo at right). That's because you use the same pattern to create both the inlay itself and the recess that it fits into.

What's really nice about these systems is that you can inlay just about any design as long as all inside corners have a radius over a set length. For the Freud inlay system shown here, the minimum radius is $9/32$".

Make and attach the template
Make your template from $1/4$"-thick quality plywood so it extends roughly 3" to 5" around the perimeter of the template guide. The template should be $1/2$" larger on the perimeter than the inlay, as the template guide rides on the inside edge of the template. Also, no part of the pattern can be smaller than $9/32$"; otherwise the template guide will not be able to pass through. Attach the template to the workpiece with clamps (middle photo) or double-sided carpet tape.

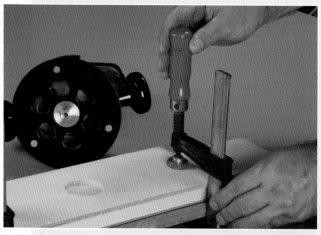

Rout the recess
Attach the template guide to the bit opening in your router's base plate. (Note: Some routers may require a universal adapter ring to accept the template guide; the router or inlay system manufacturer usually sells these.) Insert the bit provided with the system and set it to the desired depth. Then turn the router on and plunge the bit into the workpiece. Follow the inside pattern of the template and then remove the waste inside the pattern (bottom photo). You can use the same bit, but as it's small, you may want to switch to a larger straight bit to remove the bulk of the waste.

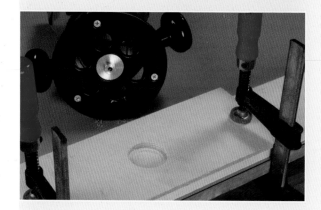

Remove the collar

Now remove the small adapter bushing that fits over the guide bushing, and set the router depth to cut through the inlay material (top photo). Attach the inlay material to a scrap of wood with double-sided carpet tape. Make sure the area under the inlay is taped to prevent it from moving once cut free and damaging the inlay. Note: The inlay material should be slightly thicker than the depth of the recess; this will let you sand it flush once it's installed.

Rout the inlay

To rout the inlay, turn on the router and, keeping the bushing against the inside edge of the template, plunge the bit into the inlay material. Now you can carefully follow the inside of the template around its perimeter to cut the inlay to shape (middle photo). Keep the bushing firmly pressed against the inside edge. When you reach the end of the cut, hold the router in place and turn it off. Let the bit stop completely before you lift out the router. Removing the router before the bit stops will ding the edge and ruin the inlay. Note: If you're using a plunge router, simply release the locking lever to allow the motor unit to return to its start position.

Add the inlay

All that's left is to free the inlay from the scrap wood and install it (bottom photo). Don't pry the inlay off the scrap or you may break the thin inlay. Instead, drizzle a little lacquer thinner under the inlay to dissolve the tape's adhesive and gently lift the inlay out. Apply a thin layer of glue inside the recess and insert the inlay. It should fit perfectly. If needed, use a wood block and a rubber mallet to tap it in place gently. Finally, sand it smooth.

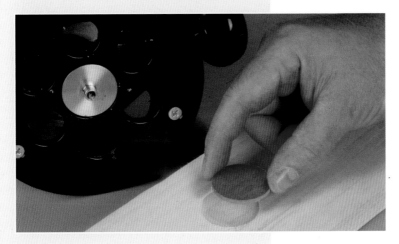

Inlay Strips

If you don't want to invest in an inlay system (see pages 64–65), you can still add inlays to your work. Decorative inlay strips are easily made with a router fitted with a straight bit and an edge guide. The inlay strips can be cut from contrasting wood and can provide a nice accent to any project. There are a couple of techniques for getting a good fit between the inlay and the recess it fits in. Always cut the inlay so it will stand proud once installed, then sand it flush with the surface (top drawing). Since router bits come in set diameters, it's best to rout the recess first and then cut the inlay to fit.

Set up for the cut

To rout the recess, begin by fitting the desired bit in the router. Attach an edge guide and an auxiliary fence (top photo), and set the fence away from the bit the desired setback from the edge of the workpiece.

Rout the recess

Now rout the recess for the inlay. For large pieces, it's best to clamp stop blocks (see page 63) near the corners to stop the recess precisely. Turn the router on and, with the edge guide pressed firmly against the edge of the workpiece, gently lower the router into the workpiece. As soon as the router's base plate is flat on the workpiece, start guiding it along the edge, taking care to stop at the corners (middle photo).

Add the inlay

Inlay strips can be bought in a variety of widths, or you can make your own. On a table saw, hold the inlay material on edge and cut a kerf so it will produce the desired thickness. Then set the rip fence up to cut through the inlay to the desired width. Make sure to cut the inlay so the waste falls safely away from the blade. Once it's cut to size, apply a light coat of glue to the recess and gently tap the inlay in place. Corners should be mitered for best appearance.

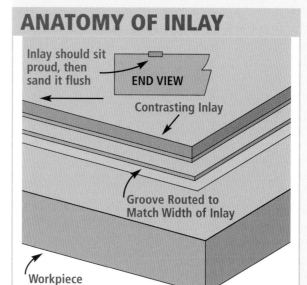

ANATOMY OF INLAY

Inlay should sit proud, then sand it flush

END VIEW

Contrasting Inlay

Groove Routed to Match Width of Inlay

Workpiece

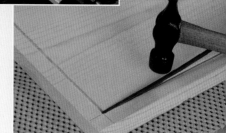

ANATOMY OF A HALF-LAP

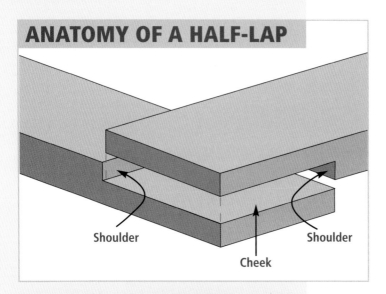

Shoulder

Shoulder

Cheek

Lap Joints

A lap joint is formed whenever two parts are lapped over one another. In furniture construction, both ends of the pieces are usually notched so the surfaces end up flush with one another — this joint is technically called a half-lap and does an excellent job of resisting lateral movement. Half-laps are commonly used to join frame pieces together and are widely used in solid-wood furniture construction.

Clamp pieces next to each other

Half-laps of any size are very easy to cut with a portable router. To provide as stable a platform as possible for the router base, it's best to clamp the workpieces side by side, as shown in the photo at left. Then all you need do is set up a stop to define the shoulders of the half-laps. To do this, first draw a line on the workpieces to indicate the shoulder. Then fit a straight bit in the router and place it on the workpiece so the bit is directly above the marked line. Next, clamp a stop to the workpieces, taking care to position it so it's perpendicular to the edge of the workpiece.

Rout the joint

Before you make your cut, it's a good idea to make a few tests on scrap the same thickness as your workpieces to identify the desired depth of cut. An easy way to do this is to make a cut through the middle of a piece of scrap. Then cut it in half at the cut. Flip one piece over and press the two cut edges together. If the bit depth is correct, the surface of the scraps will be flush. Once set, you can rout the half-laps (bottom photo). Start at the end of the workpiece and work back toward the stop, taking light cuts along the full width of the workpiece. This is a good time to rout the edges, as this will help prevent chip-out. When the router base hits the stop, you're done.

Mortising

Without a doubt, the mortise-and-tenon is one of the strongest joints in furniture construction. That's why it's used almost exclusively for joining together high-stress or high-load parts, such as the sides of a chair or bench. The mortise-and-tenon has two parts: a hole (usually square) called a mortise is made in one part, and a tenon is cut on the end of the mating part. Tenons are cut by removing wood on all four sides at the end of the part, creating shoulders. The tenon fits into the mortise and can be glued in place or held via dowels, fasteners, or even a wedge.

The simplest way to get a mortise-and-tenon to fit together is to cut the mortise first, then cut the tenon to fit. That's because it's much easier to resize a tenon than it is to recut a mortise. Mortises may be round or square, centered or offset, and stopped or through (see the top drawing below). Although there are stand-alone mortising machines, they're expensive. A low-cost alternative is to make a mortising jig for your router (see the sidebar below).

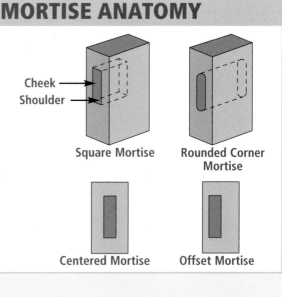

MORTISE ANATOMY

Cheek
Shoulder

Square Mortise   Rounded Corner Mortise

Centered Mortise   Offset Mortise

SIMPLE MORTISING JIG

One of the easiest ways to cut mortises is to make a mortising jig for your router (see the drawing at right). The jig replaces your existing router base and houses a pair of cutoff bolts that guide the router during its cut. The beauty of this jig is that it's self-centering. That is, as long as you keep the bolts pressed up against the sides of the workpiece during a cut, the mortise will be routed in the exact center of the workpiece.

To make the jig, cut a piece of ¼" Plexiglas, MDF (medium-density fiberboard), or plywood to match your original base. Use your original base to mark the hole for the bit and the holes for the mounting screws, and drill appropriate-sized holes. Then mark one diagonal and measure 1⅝" out from the center in each direction; drill a pair of ⅜" holes. You'll need to counterbore these so the heads of the bolts will be flush with the surface. All that's left is to cut the threads off of two 3¼"-long, ⅜"-diameter stove bolts with a hacksaw. File the ends smooth and glue the bolts in the counterbored holes with epoxy. Once it's set, attach the jig to your router and you're ready to go.

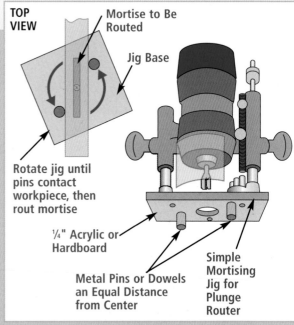

TOP VIEW

Mortise to Be Routed

Jig Base

Rotate jig until pins contact workpiece, then rout mortise

¼" Acrylic or Hardboard

Metal Pins or Dowels an Equal Distance from Center

Simple Mortising Jig for Plunge Router

Set up the router

To use the mortising jig, first insert the desired diameter bit into the collet (either a straight bit or a spiral-mill bit, see page 30 for more on these bits). Tighten the bit and set the depth stop or stops on the router for the desired depth of cut. Then mark the ends of the mortise on the workpiece with a try square and a pencil (above). Because of the self-centering nature of the mortising jig, all you need to mark are the ends of the mortise.

Add the stops

You could rout the mortise right now, but it's often difficult to see the end of mortise lines you've drawn on the workpiece, so it's easy to go past them. A way to prevent this and ensure an accurate mortise is to clamp some stop blocks to the workpiece. Just slide the router over until the bit is positioned at the end of the mortise, then clamp a block to the workpiece. Note that since the jig is rotated in use to keep the bolts pressed up against the workpiece, the stop blocks will be angled to match (middle photo).

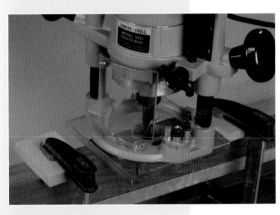

Rout the mortise in passes

Now place the router and jig on the workpiece and pivot the unit until both bolts butt up against the sides of the workpiece. Position the router bit (either a straight bit or a spiral mill bit) at the top mark. Turn on the router and lower the bit into the workpiece about $1/4$". Keeping the bolts pressed firmly against the sides of the workpiece, slowly pull the router forward until you reach the other mark. Turn off the router, raise the bit, and return to the start. Continue making passes until the full mortise depth is reached.

Routing Tenons

As mentioned on page 68, most woodworkers find that it's easier to make tenons to fit mortises than the other way around. And just like mortises, tenons may be square, round, centered, offset, stopped or through (see the drawing on page 68). In most cases, you'll find that rounding over the tenons to match routed mortises is simpler than squaring up mortises; for more on fitting mortise-and-tenon joints, see page 110.

Add a stop
Routing a tenon with a portable router is very similar to routing half-laps (see page 67). As with half-laps, if you need to rout more than one tenon, it's best to clamp the workpieces side by side to make a more stable platform for the router base. Alternatively, consider clamping the pieces end to end (see page 71). To define the shoulder of the tenon accurately, clamp a scrap of wood to the workpiece to serve as a stop (middle photo). Use a try square to ensure that the stop is perpendicular to the edge of the workpiece.

Rout the end
Once you've set the router for the desired depth of cut, place it on the end of the workpiece and turn it on. Then gently ease the bit in the end of the workpiece. Take a light, full-width cut and then rout lightly along both side edges of the tenon to help prevent chip-out. Keep taking light passes, working toward the stop. Routing this way will provide the most stable platform for the router base.

ANATOMY OF A TENON

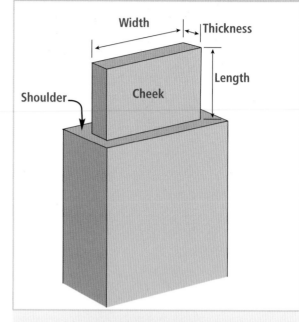

Width | Thickness | Length | Shoulder | Cheek

Work toward the stop

As you get near the stop, slow down a bit and take even lighter passes. This will prevent chip-out and help keep the router from bouncing or chattering along the stop once it makes contact. Once you're done with one face, flip the workpiece (or workpieces) over and rout the other side. If the tenon has four shoulders and you need to rout the workpiece on edge, see page 57 for a tip on supporting the workpiece safely.

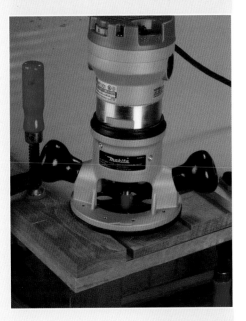

Add support at the end

Another way to stabilize a cut near the end of a workpiece is to add a scrap block to support the end of the router base that extends past the end of the workpiece (middle photo). The only critical thing here is that the scrap block must be the same thickness as the workpiece, or else you'll rout a tapered tenon. Choose a long scrap so you can clamp it in place; this way the clamp won't interfere with the router.

Clamp the workpieces back to back

A final trick for routing tenons is to clamp the pieces to be routed end-to-end as shown in the photo below. This is similar to the tip shown above, except instead of using a separate support block, each workpiece serves as a support block for the other.

Routing Dovetails

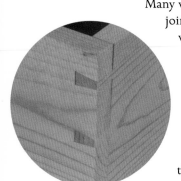

Many woodworkers view the dovetail joint as the ultimate way to join wood. The joint is both attractive and incredibly strong (see the photo at left). The joint gets its name from the tail half of the joint that resembles the shape of a dove's tail (see the drawing at right). The other half of the joint is the pins, which fit into the openings between the tails.

Cutting precise dovetails by hand requires a steady hand, a keen eye, and razor-sharp tools — not to mention considerable practice. Cutting precise dovetails with a router fitted with a dovetail bit is simple when using a quality dovetail jig.

There are numerous dovetail jigs on the market that can cut different types of dovetail joints; the most common cut half-blind and/or through dovetails. Half-blind dovetails are commonly used to join drawer sides to drawer fronts. This is because the mechanical strength of the joint gained from the interlocking pins and tails stands up well to the day-to-day pushing and pulling stresses a drawer is subjected to. The half-blind dovetail joint is hidden when the drawer is closed. When you want the dovetails to show, you use through dovetails. Through dovetails are routinely used to join together parts of a cabinet or chest.

The instructions shown here are for cutting through dovetails with the Akeda dovetail jig. As technique varies from jig to jig, make sure to read and follow the manufacturer's directions. As with many jigs, the Akeda provides built-in clamps to hold the work-pieces secure. The Akeda also offers tracks that accept pin and tail templates; spacing is variable in 1/8" increments. All dovetail jigs are designed to work with a router fitted with a guide bushing. The guide bushing is pressed against the pin and tail guides in use to cut the pins and tails.

Set up the jig

In order to clamp the workpieces, most dovetail jigs are designed to extend past the edge of the bench or work surface where they're clamped. Some jigs require you to make a clamping base and fasten it to the jig, as shown below. Make sure the jig openings clear the front edge of the bench when you clamp it.

ANATOMY OF A DOVETAIL

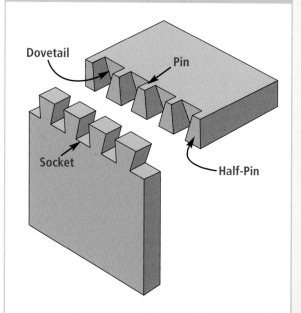

Dovetail · Pin · Socket · Half-Pin

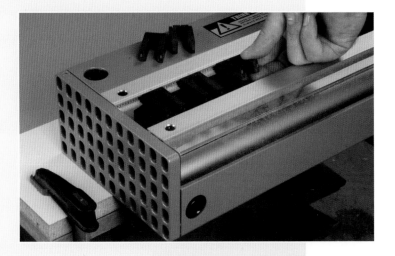

Insert the tail guides

Consult the instructions for your jig to determine which part of the joint you should cut first. The Akeda system shown here recommends cutting the tails first. With this system, you simply select the tail spacing you want and then snap the tail guides into the track, as shown in the top photo. Most systems offer spacing in $1/8$" to $1/4$" increments. Other systems provide precut templates, where the pin spacing is not adjustable.

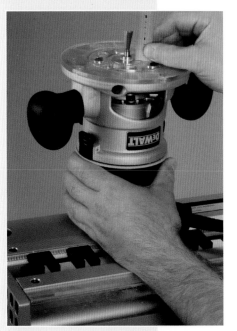

Set up the dovetail bit

Some dovetail jigs come with their own special bits; others use standard bits. One nice thing about the Akeda system shown here is that not only does it come with all the bits you'll need, but it also comes with fractionally larger and smaller bits that can be used to fine-tune the fit. Follow the manufacturer's directions for installing the guide bushing and adjusting the dovetail bit height. A test cut in scrap wood is strongly advised: it's tough to adjust the bit by eye to the precise setting needed.

Clamp the first workpiece

With the router all set up, you can insert the workpiece in the jig that will end up with the tails. Follow the jig placement directions carefully. Most will have a pre-set or adjustable stop that the side of the workpiece should butt up against. The end of the workpiece typically butts gently up against the pin guides or template. When in place, use the built-in clamping system to secure the workpiece (bottom photo). On the Akeda system shown here, this is simply a matter of turning a single knob.

Rout the tails

Now you're ready for the fun part — routing the tails. Place the router on the jig so the bit is away from the workpiece. Then turn on the router and slide the router over until it reaches the first tail guide. Gently guide the router forward until the guide bushing contacts the tail guide and the bit bites into the workpiece (top photo). Press the router bit into the wood, taking care to listen to the sound of the motor. If the tone lowers considerably as you press forward, your feed rate is too fast. Ease off a little and continue pressing until the bit nears the end of the cut. Then ease off considerably to prevent chip-out as the bit exits the wood. Pull the router clear of the tail guide and move on to the next guide. Continue like this until all tails are cut.

Insert the pin guides

With the tails cut, loosen the built-in clamp and remove the first workpiece. Vacuum out any dust and chips and then insert the pin guides (see the middle photo at right). These will be placed with the same spacing as the tails. With half-blind dovetails, you'll typically use the same template to cut both halves of the joint.

Insert the second workpiece

Following the manufacturer's directions, insert the second workpiece that will be routed to form the pins. Here again, it's important to follow the specific directions for your jig, since you may or may not need to offset the workpiece. Most jigs will have you butt the edge up against a stop and the end of the workpiece up against the pin guides or template. Secure the workpiece with the built-in clamp or clamps (bottom photo).

Set up the straight bit

Unlike the tails, the sides of the pins are not angled. They're perfectly parallel with the edge of the workpiece when viewed from its face. When viewed from the end, though, they are angled to match the angle of the tails. The pins are cut with a straight bit, using the same guide bushing used to cut the tails. Insert the bit in the router and adjust the bit according to the manufacturer's directions (top photo).

Rout the pins

Because you'll be removing a considerable amount of material when you rout the pins, it's best to hook up a shop vacuum to the jig if possible. Rout the pins as you did the tails by pressing the guide bushing up against the pin guides. Take care to ease up on the pressure as the bit exits the workpiece. Work side to side, taking light cuts to remove the majority of the waste between the pins (middle photo).

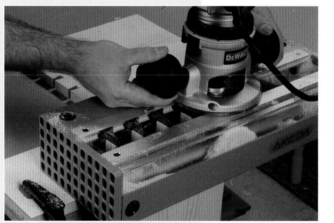

Test the fit

After the pins have been routed, remove the workpiece and test the fit of the joint by inserting the pins in the tails and pressing gently down (bottom photo). If they don't fit, don't force them. Adjust the jig as necessary or use the modified bits provided to fine-tune the fit. The two halves of the joint should go together with firm hand pressure alone. If you have to reach for a mallet, the fit needs to be adjusted.

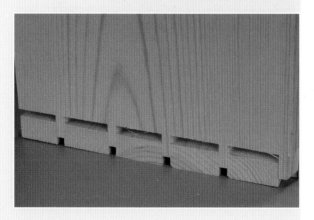

Sliding Dovetail

A variation of the dovetail joint that's extremely useful in carcase construction is the sliding dovetail.

This joint is especially well suited for joining web frames to the sides of a cabinet or dresser: The mechanical strength alone is enough to hold the parts together. No glue is necessary here, only a single pin to keep the joint from sliding out of position. This is very important in a cabinet or chest where the grain of the web frame runs perpendicular to the grain of the sides — as it does in most cabinets. Because the two parts will expand and contract at different rates due to the difference in grain orientation, gluing the two together would eventually cause the side to split.

The beauty of the sliding dovetail is that it holds the parts together yet allows them to expand and contract at their own rate. The joint's tail actually slides within the pin, hence the name. The tail, cut on the edge of a workpiece, fits into a long single pin recess cut in the face of a workpiece (drawing at right). Sliding dovetails can be either through or stopped.

Set up a guide
Since the width of the notch you'll be cutting will depend on the router bit you're using, it's best to rout the pin recess first and then rout the tail to fit. To rout the pin recess, start by clamping a straightedge to the workpiece to serve as a guide (middle photo). Make sure the guide is perpendicular to the edge of the workpiece and positioned so the dovetail bit is directly over the location of the recess to be routed. Alternatively, you can use a guide bushing and simply offset the guide the required amount.

Rout the pin recess
Depending on the depth of the pin recess (length of

the pin), you may or may not be able to make the cut in one pass. Depths less than $1/2$" are usually fine to take in one pass (bottom photo). Anything deeper would be easier to rout if you first took a pass with a straight bit to remove the majority of the waste. Be careful to ease up on feed pressure as the bit exits the wood to prevent chip-out (you could also clamp a scrap block to the edge as described on page 55).

SLIDING DOVETAIL ANATOMY

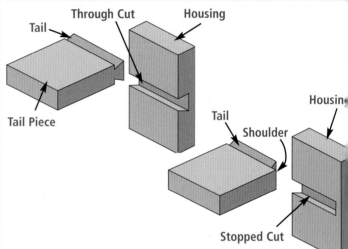

Tail • Through Cut • Housing • Tail Piece • Tail • Shoulder • Housing • Stopped Cut

Adjust the edge guide

The long tail can be routed with the same bit. Because you're routing the end of the workpiece, it's important to clamp a support block to the piece to be routed to stabilize the cut; for more on this, see page 57. To guide the bit, attach an edge guide to the router, fitted with a long auxiliary fence (top photo). Then adjust the bit for the desired tail width. Take a practice cut on scrap to make sure the tail is the correct dimension.

Rout the long, single tail

Once the router is set up and the bit is adjusted, go ahead and make the tail cuts, one on each side of the workpiece, as shown in the middle photo. To prevent tearing-out the face of the workpiece, take a very light first pass so the bottom edge of the bit will just sever the wood fibers on the face of the workpiece.

Test the fit

With both sides of the joint cut, it's time to test the fit. As with the standard dovetail, the sliding dovetail joint should go together with firm hand pressure. If you need a mallet to drive the parts together, the fit is too tight; shave a little off the pin recess and try again.

Even when fit properly, these joints tend to be finicky. Don't slide the joint together fully until you're ready to assemble the project parts, or you may not be able to get the parts apart without damaging them. That's because the wood toward the center of any board has a higher moisture content than the surface. When you slide the tail into the "wet" pin recess, the dryer tail absorbs moisture and will swell up, locking the two parts together.

Router Trimming

Trimming plastic laminate with a flush-trim bit is a natural for many woodworkers. But did you realize you could use a router to trim other things? A router and a little imagination can make quick work of trimming plugs perfectly flush and even removing dried glue. And when fitted with a flush-trim bit, a router can quickly trim edging to size.

Routing plugs flush

If you've ever spent time trying to trim wood plugs with a chisel so they end up flush with the surface without marring it, you'll appreciate this simple technique. Fit your router with a $1/2$" or $3/4$" straight bit, then fasten a couple of same-thickness scraps to the bottom of the router base, as shown in the top photo, with double-sided carpet tape. Then adjust the bit so it's barely above the surface. Turn on the router and guide it gently over the plug, taking light passes.

Removing glue squeeze-out

Glue squeeze-out can be very frustrating to remove once the glue has dried. Using a chisel or a scraper inevitably leads to wood fibers being torn out and the surface being damaged. To remove dried glue, you can use a technique similar to that described above for routing plugs flush (middle photo). The only difference in technique is that it's best to remove the glue in a series of lighter passes, lowering the bit slightly after each pass until it just glides over the work surface.

Trimming edging strips

It seems that edging strips never seem to glue on flush to an edge. So most woodworkers cut the strips a bit wide and then plane or scrape them to width. The problem with either of these techniques is that it's easy to damage the surface with a plane iron or a scraper. A simpler approach that won't ding the surface is to use a router and a flush-trim bit, as shown.

Laminate trimmers work best for this, as it's easier to keep the base flat on the narrow edge (bottom photo). For a more stable cut, see the tip on page 57.

Duplicating Parts

A router is the perfect tool to make duplicate parts, especially curved parts like the delicately curved arms for a set of chairs or the arched slats for a garden bench. This simple technique entails making a pattern and using this to duplicate the parts. The pattern or template is often made from 1/4" hardboard since its smooth surface and dense edges make it perfect for running a bearing along its edge. The best bit for the job is a patternmaker's bit, described in the sidebar below.

Attach the pattern to the blank

There are a couple of ways to attach a template to a workpiece. One is to affix it with double-sided tape (top photo). This works fine for a few pieces, but if you're duplicating a lot of parts, it's worth the time to make a jig to hold the parts as they're routed. The jig not only holds the part in place, but the edge also serves as the template. Fast-action toggle clamps are a great way to secure the parts to the jig while still letting you quickly remove and change the part.

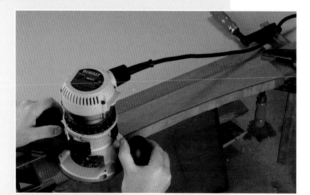

Rout the blank

Once you've attached the template or pattern to the blank, remove as much waste as possible before pattern-routing. A band saw or saber saw works best for this. The idea is to leave around 1/16" to 1/8" waste along the pattern's edge. Then secure the blank to your bench or work surface with clamps. Set the patternmaker's bit so the bearing rides along the edge of the pattern and the cutting edge can trim the full thickness of the blank in a single pass. Turn on the router and run the bit gently along the template to duplicate the curve (middle photo).

HOW IT WORKS

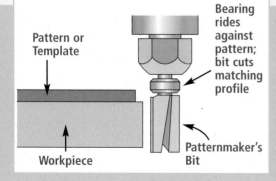

Pattern or Template

Bearing rides against pattern; bit cuts matching profile

Workpiece

Patternmaker's Bit

PATTERNMAKER'S BIT

The key to easy patternmaking is a special router bit called a patternmaker's bit. It's basically a straight bit with a bearing mounted on top; the bearing is the same diameter as the bit. By attaching a template to the top of a workpiece, you can guide the bearing along the edge of the template and the straight bit will trim the workpiece to the identical shape of the template.

Mortising Hinges

Another example of a router's versatility is using it to accurately rout mortises for hinges. Unless you're highly skilled with a chisel — and even if you are — you have to admire the speed and efficiency with which a router can tackle the shallow mortises required for most hinges. Although you can purchase hinge-mortising jigs — and they're well worth the money if you need to rout a lot of them — you can get the job done with a couple of stops and a router fitted with a straight bit.

Lay out the hinge

The simplest way to accurately lay out the hinge on the workpiece is to use the hinge itself as a pattern. Just flip one flap of the hinge over and position the hinge at the desired location. Press the hinge against the workpiece until the flipped hinge flap butts up against the side of the workpiece, as shown in the top photo. Then simply trace around the hinge flap.

Add the stops

You could rout the mortise now, but it's a lot safer to add stops to limit the router's travel. Place the router over the marked hinge at the ends or limits of the hinge, then slide a stop over to butt against the side of the router base. Clamp the stop in place and repeat for the other side (see the middle photo at right).

Rout the mortise

Set the straight bit for the desired depth of cut, and place the router on top of the workpiece with the bit away from the edge. Turn on the router and gently ease the bit into the workpiece. Make the end cuts first, then remove the waste between these cuts (bottom photo). At the back edge of the hinge flap, stay about $1/16$" away from the marked line. Turn off the router and test the fit. Remove any excess waste with a chisel, and square up the corners if necessary.

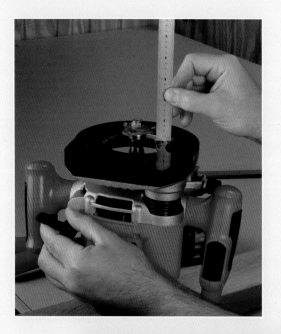

Routing Slots

Occasionally a project calls for a slot to be cut in the edge of a board, most often to accept a spline to join the piece to another. Although you can do this on a router table, you'd need to hold the workpiece on edge. This often leads to inaccurate cuts, since the workpiece will tend to wobble if not pressed firmly up against a fence. A simpler, more accurate way to cut slots is to rout them with a slot cutter (see page 32 for more on these bits). The cut is more accurate because you make it with the workpiece lying flat.

Set up the bit

To rout a slot, start by inserting a slot cutter into the router. Since these are typically large in diameter, it won't fit in the bit opening and you'll have to install it from above. Once you've tightened the bit securely in the collet, use a metal rule or tape measure to set the cutter to the desired cut location (top photo).

Rout the slot

Before you rout the actual slot, make a test cut or two to verify that the slot is in the correct position and the desired depth. If you want the slot to be shallower than the full depth, attach an edge guide to the router and set it for the desired depth. Once the location is confirmed, place the router on the workpiece, turn on the router, and rout the slot (middle photo).

Add a spline

If the part you've slotted is to be joined to another, cut a spline to width. In most cases you'll want the width of the spline to be about $1/16$" narrower than the combined width of the slots to leave room for glue. Since most slot cutters are made in $1/8$" increments, you can usually find hardboard or plywood to fit snug in the slot (bottom photo). If you do use solid wood, make sure the grain direction of the spline is *perpendicular* to the grain of the pieces to be joined. If it's parallel, the spline will easily split if stressed.

Laminate Trimmers

Many woodworkers feel a laminate trimmer is something only a countertop or cabinet installer would use, but that isn't so. The size of these peppy little machines makes them extremely handy for use on almost any project, because they can get into places a fixed-base router can't — and they can access areas a plunge router can only dream about. Also, their small size is better suited to routing small pieces that would be dwarfed by a larger router. Sure, they're not designed to hog off lots of wood; but in many cases, they're the only tool that can get the job done.

Basic technique

Laminate trimmers were designed to remove excess laminate from projects. When fitted with a flush-trim bit, they excel at it. Just plunge the bit through the laminate until the bearing hits the workpiece and then continue routing, with the bearing pressed along the workpiece edge (top photo). Since there are no handles on a laminate trimmer, just grab the motor unit and go.

Laminate trimmers also work great for profiling edges. The only limitation you'll find is that most accept only $1/4$" bits, and the bit opening in the base limits the size of the bit you can install. Larger bits, like the chamfer bit shown here, can cut only slight chamfers before the bit hits the router base. If you need a deeper cut, make a throw-away replacement base and cut the opening as large as you need.

Standard versus an offset base

To give laminate trimmers an even greater ability to go where no other router can, manufacturers have created offset bases that basically shift the cut-

ting ability closer to the edge; see the drawing below. This lets a laminate trimmer rout almost (not quite all the way) into a corner.

OFFSET AND STANDARD BASES

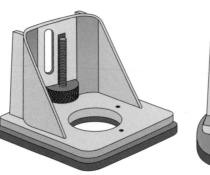

Standard Base

Offset Base

Sign Making

Sign-making jigs, like the one shown here manufactured by Craftsman, have been extremely popular over the years. This and similar sign-making jigs are easy to use and come with various fonts so you can create the look you're after. In addition to offering different fonts — or typefaces — the letter templates also come in various sizes. Virtually all sign-making jigs require that the router be fitted with a guide bushing of a specific diameter to fit into the letter templates and guide the router to shape the letter.

Typically, the first step to using one of these is to assemble the jig from the supplied parts. Most jigs consist of a pair of extruded bars that fit into clamp bodies (drawing). Letter guides slide into channels in the bars. An adjustable stop on one end is slid over and tightened to keep the letter templates from shifting in use. A pair of clamping rods pass through clamp bodies and are fitted with a fixed and adjustable clamp pad at each end. These are fitted over the workpiece and hold the jig in place.

SIGN-MAKING JIG

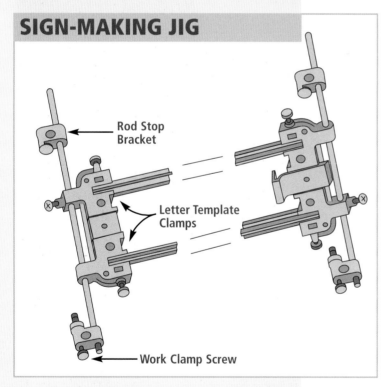

Rod Stop Bracket

Letter Template Clamps

Work Clamp Screw

How it works

In use, the guide bushing of the router slips into the opening in the letter guide and then is pushed along the guide to form the letter. You can rout the letters with either a straight bit or a core-box bit, as long as the bit fits inside the bushing.

Insert the letter templates

To use the sign-making jig, first select the letters of the word you want to spell. Blank templates are usually provided to fill in between words or as fillers. Loosen the guide clamp screws and pull one of the clamp bodies off the extruded bars. Then slip the letter templates into the channels in the bars (top photo). Next, replace the clamp body and loosen the stop (middle photo). Now slide it over to press the templates firmly in place.

Position the jig on the workpiece

Locate and mark the place on the workpiece where you want the first letter to begin. Align the front edge of the jig with the front edge of the workpiece so they're parallel to each other.

Clamp the jig in place

To secure the jig, loosen the screws on the clamp pads and slide them on the rods until the nylon buttons on the pads butt up against the workpiece. Then tighten the screws on the clamp pads and twist the knob on the adjustable clamp pad until the jig is securely locked in place (bottom photo).

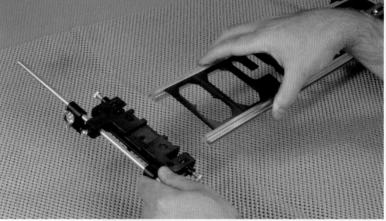

Add the bushing to the router

Most sign-making kits supply the bushing needed to fit the letter templates. Others don't, so it's always smart to have a universal bushing set on hand (see page 35). Follow the manufacturer's directions to install the bushing in the router base. Some are designed to fit in the opening and are secured with a threaded collar. Other bushings (like the one shown at left) are attached to the router base with screws. As there's often some play in this, install a straight bit to make sure there's an even gap between the bit and the guide bushing around its entire perimeter.

Install the bit and set depth

If you haven't already installed the bit of your choice, do so now. Then set the bit height (middle photo). If you're planning on routing letters deeper than $1/4$", make multiple, lighter passes. Core-box bits can usually be set to the full depth, since the rounded ends remove less wood than a straight bit.

Rout the letters

You're finally ready to rout the letters. Lower the guide bushing gently into the groove in the letter template, making sure to keep the bushing constantly in contact with the letter template. Start the router and lower the spinning bit into the wood (bottom photo). As soon as you begin cutting, move the router to prevent burning. When the letter is complete, turn off the router and raise it off the jig. A plunge router makes this operation a whole lot easier, as you can plunge down at the beginning of the cut and then allow it to raise back up at the end. Repeat for the remaining letters.

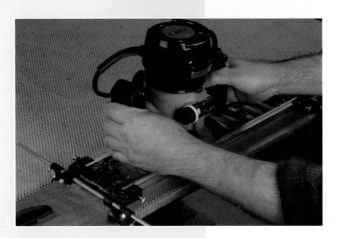

4 Table-Mounted Router Techniques

Whoever first thought of mounting a router upside-down in a table deserves a universal woodworker's appreciation medal. That's because this simple concept basically turns your router into a shaper capable of producing intricate joinery not possible with a handheld router — things like cope-and-stick frames with raised panels and box joints.

Additionally, a table-mounted router lets you add a lot of tricks to your woodworking bag, such as making your own dowels, safely routing small pieces, and duplicating patterns with a pin arm. But that's not to say a table-mounted router is good only for tricky work. If you've never used one before, you'll quickly discover that next to your table saw, it's likely to be the most-used tool in your shop. Why? It's so easy to quickly round over and chamfer edges and rout a wide variety of joinery, ranging from simple dadoes and rabbets to more complex joints like the mortise-and-tenon.

Mounting a router to a table is like buying a sophisticated joint-making machine, but at a fraction of the cost. You'll be able to rout box joints, mortise-and-tenon joints — even make frame-and-panel doors. If you don't have a router table, consider buying one (see pages 36–37) or making one (see pages 149–155).

Basic Technique

With a table-mounted router, you present the workpiece to the router instead of the other way around (see the photo below right). This offers a number of advantages. For starters, it virtually eliminates the need for clamping the workpiece, since you're holding it and guiding it past the bit. Moving the workpiece instead of a top-heavy router also gives you better control while giving an excellent view of the bit. By adding a fence, you can guide a workpiece past the bit effortlessly, with precision. The only disadvantage you'll find with a table-mounted router is that it can be challenging to rout a large piece. In such cases, you're better off with a handheld router.

Feed direction

As with a handheld router, there are rules to be followed concerning feed direction and feed rate. For most routing operations, you'll want to feed the workpiece into the router from right to left, as shown in the drawing below. Feeding the workpiece like this will make the rotating bit pull the workpiece into the fence. Likewise, if you're routing without a fence and using a piloted bit with a bearing instead, the bit rotation will pull the workpiece into the bearing. In both cases, bit rotation is working for you by making it easier to keep contact between the workpiece and the guide — either the fence or the bearing. If you were to reverse the feed direction, the bit rotation would force the workpiece away from the guide. As with a handheld router, this is backrouting and can be extremely dangerous on a table-mounted router. That's because it's easy for the bit to grab the workpiece and pull your hands into the bit. For the most part, backrouting should not be done on a table-mounted router; for an exception, see page 101.

Feed rate

Just like a hand-held router, the rate at which a bit meets the workpiece, or a workpiece meets the bit as here, will have a big impact on the quality of the cut. The rate at which you feed the workpiece into the spinning bit, or feed rate, should allow the bit to remove wood at a steady rate without overloading the motor. As long as your bits are clean and sharp (see pages 174–175 for more on this), you'll be able to identify proper feed rate by listening to the router's motor. If you detect a definite drop in the tone, you're probably feeding the workpiece too fast. Unfortunately, some routers with powerful motors are tough to bog down; the only indication of an overly fast feed rate is a profiled edge or cut that isn't smooth — instead, the edge will be scalloped. If this happens, simply run the workpiece past the bit again with a slower feed rate. A feed rate that's too slow will exhibit burning, and often a rough cut, too.

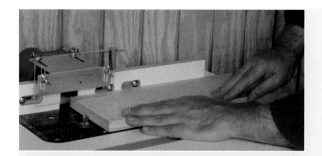

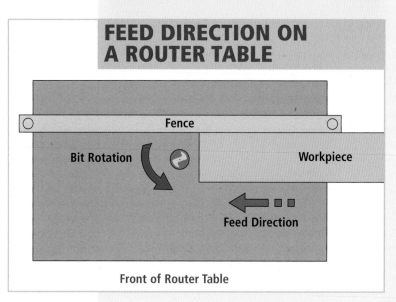

FEED DIRECTION ON A ROUTER TABLE

Fence

Bit Rotation

Workpiece

Feed Direction

Front of Router Table

SETTING BIT HEIGHT

How you adjust the height of the bit in your table-mounted router will depend on your router. The bit-height mechanism on a fixed-base router is adjusted just as it is for handheld operation; for more on this, see pages 50–51. But because the router is mounted under a table, there's more of a challenge setting the bit to the desired height: One hand needs to hold some sort of measuring device while the other adjusts the bit height. This is one reason you'll be better off mounting the router to a router plate that fits in a recess in the top; ease of changing bits is the other reason.

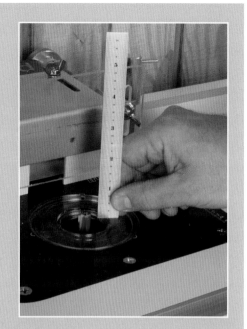

Setting height with a ruler. A small metal rule, like the one shown in the top photo at right, is an easy way to roughly position the bit height. Once the height is locked in place, make a test cut and check the depth. If necessary, readjust bit height and continue making test cuts until you've snuck up on the desired depth.

Setting height with a gauge. For more accurate positioning, consider adjusting bit height with a simple shop-made gauge, like the one shown at right. (For directions on how to make this gauge, see page 51.) Set the gauge to the desired bit height and then position it over the bit opening. Then raise the bit until it just touches the gauge slide. Lock the bit in position and make a test cut; adjust as necessary.

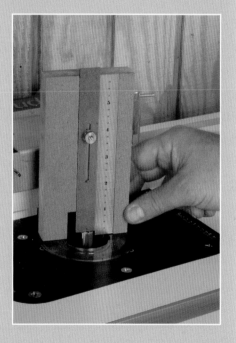

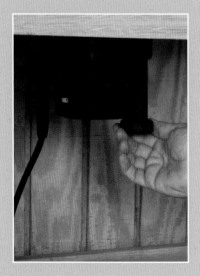

Setting height with an extension knob. Plunge routers are the easiest table-mounted routers to adjust because all you have to do is reach up and turn a knob (see the photo at left). If your router doesn't have one of these, you can purchase an extension for most brands that will bring the knob down so it's readily accessible; see page 41 for more on these. Note: Although an extension knob makes raising and lowering the bit a simple one-handed operation, you'll still need to use a rule or a gauge and test cuts as described above to set the bit to the desired height.

Freehand Routing

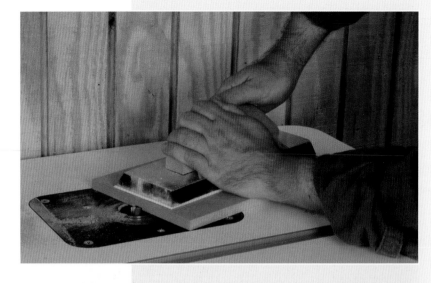

Get a grip

The most important thing to remember if you need to rout freehand on a table-mounted router is to have a solid grip on the workpiece — one where there's no chance that your fingers could come in contact with the spinning bit. The reason this is critical relates to how a bit cuts when it's embedded in wood. Unlike a non-piloted bit that's used with a fence and is pulled into the fence by the bit's rotation, the rotating bit in a non-guided cut will tend to follow the grain of the wood. That's because there's no fence to guide it, so it'll take the path of least resistance. In most wood, this means the bit will try to follow the less dense, fast-growing early wood sandwiched between layers of harder, slow-growing late wood. So if you have an intended path for the bit, you have to have a very secure hold on the work-piece. For safety, it's best to grip

the workpiece with a rubber grout float, as shown in the top photo. A grout float will grip the wood well and keep your hands out of harm's way.

Removing waste

A common reason to freehand rout on a table-mounted router is to remove waste, as when routing a recess as shown in the middle photo. What makes this tricky is that feed direction varies relative to how the bit is oriented to the recess. The only way to find out which direction to feed is to start routing. If the bit grabs the workpiece, reverse direction. As always, light cuts are safer and will produce cleaner cuts.

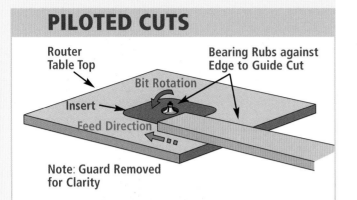

Router Table Top

Bearing Rubs against Edge to Guide Cut

Bit Rotation

Insert

Feed Direction

Note: Guard Removed for Clarity

Routing with Piloted Bits

Routing with a piloted bit on a table-mounted router is one of the most common operations — and by far the simplest. That's because the bearing-guided bit is in clear view and all you need do is feed the workpiece carefully into the rotating bit (see the drawing at left).

Using a starting pin

Although you can rout with a piloted bit without using a starting pin, we recommend using one — especially if you're just beginning to work with a table-mounted router. A starting pin is just a short length of steel rod that fits into a hole in the table insert or table itself (inset photo). It serves as a fulcrum point to let you safely ease the edge of the workpiece into the spinning bit, see the photo at left. To use a starting pin, begin with the workpiece pressed up against the pin and then pivot the workpiece so the edge contacts the bit. Then feed the workpiece into the bit, keeping the edge in contact with the starting pin as long as possible. Experienced woodworkers usually do without the pin, as they're used to the router and have learned the best way to present a workpiece to a bit.

Final Pass   Workpiece
Second Pass
First Pass

Bit Raised in Stages

Router Table Top

Bit Opening

MULTIPLE PASSES

Just as with a handheld router, it's always best to take multiple, light passes when working with a table-mounted router (see the drawing at left). Taking light cuts puts less of a load on the router's motor, it puts less strain on the bit and collet, and it creates cleaner, crisper profiles (see the photo at right). This is true even for larger, more powerful routers that can take a full cut with a single pass. A general rule of thumb is to make a cut in three to four equal passes. For $3/4$"-thick stock, this equates to three, $1/4$"-deep cuts.

Using a Fence

If you're not using a piloted bit, odds are you'll be using a fence to guide the workpiece past the bit (top photo). Here's where a table-mounted router clearly surpasses a handheld router. Instead of a short edge guide with a limited cut that can be tough to adjust, the fence on a table-mounted router is long to fully support the workpiece, has a much greater capacity, and is easier to adjust.

A router table fence itself will largely determine how precise it is, and how easy it is to adjust. There is a huge variety of commercially made fences to choose from (see page 39), as well as those you can make yourself (see page 156–161 for directions on how to make a fence). Look for a system that locks positively and can be adjusted with minimal effort.

Position the fence

To set up a fence once the bit is installed in the router, position the fence the desired distance away from the bit. The simplest way to do this is with a metal rule (middle photo). Experienced woodworkers will get the fence in rough position, lock down one end, and then pivot the fence for the desired

position and lock down the opposite end. Yes, this will leave the fence at an angle, but this is okay for most cuts; the sidebar below explains why.

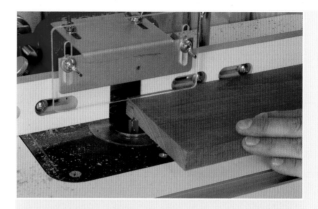

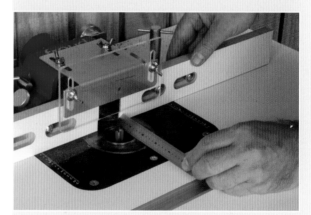

MYTH OF THE CROOKED FENCE

For most of the cuts you'll make using a fence on a table-mounted router, you should know that the fence does not have to be parallel to the edge of the table — it can be at any angle, as long as the distance between the fence and the bit is the desired amount; see the drawing. That's because regardless of the angle, the cut will be parallel to the fence. The only time a fence needs to be straight is when it's used in conjunction with a miter gauge — typically as a stop. Otherwise, the angle doesn't matter.

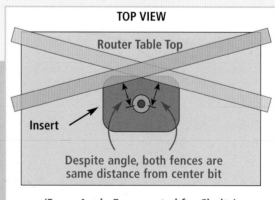

TOP VIEW

Router Table Top

Insert

Despite angle, both fences are same distance from center bit

(Fence Angle Exaggerated for Clarity)

Adjust the bit opening

Quality fences will provide some way for you to vary the opening around the bit. In general, you want the fence sections as close to the bit as possible without actually touching the bit. There are a number of reasons this is useful. First, the closer the fence face is to the bit, the more support it gives to the workpiece. Second, keeping the opening to the minimum makes it easier for fences equipped with dust control to capture and whisk away dust and chips. Finally, for cuts using a non-piloted bit (such as a straight bit), being able to fully close the bit opening helps prevent the workpiece from catching on the edge of a face (or faces) as the workpiece is fed past the bit. How you adjust the faces will depend on the fence. Some systems (like the one shown here) are held in place with screws; others use easy-to-adjust knobs.

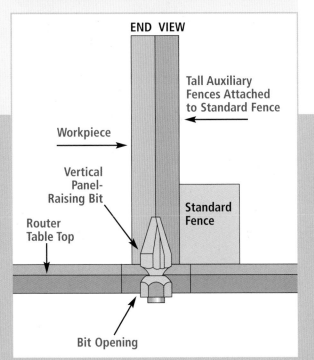

END VIEW

Tall Auxiliary Fences Attached to Standard Fence

Workpiece

Vertical Panel-Raising Bit

Standard Fence

Router Table Top

Bit Opening

TALL AUXILIARY FENCE

Often, you'll need to rout the edge of a workpiece where the cut must be made with the workpiece on edge instead of lying flat on the tabletop. The problem with this is that most fences are only 3" to 4" high: This simply is not enough to support the workpiece so it can be fed safely past the bit. That's because the workpiece will tend to tilt away from the fence as you move it along the fence. To prevent this, take the time to attach a tall auxiliary fence to your existing fence (see the photo). This is just a scrap of wood that's roughly the same height as your workpiece. Plywood and engineered panels such as MDF (medium-density fiberboard) work best here, as they're typically very flat. Attach the auxiliary fence with clamps or screws. If necessary, cut an opening for the bit. See page 94 for a simple way to create an opening to match the bit.

ZERO-CLEARANCE FENCE

As mentioned previously, it's always best to adjust fence faces so the bit opening is held to a minimum. This provides maximum support to the workpiece and allows for optimum dust collection. Additionally, if you need to rout small pieces, the smaller the opening the better, for safety. One way to do this is to make an auxiliary fence that attaches to your existing fence, see the drawing. This type of fence is commonly called a zero-clearance fence, as there's almost no space between the bit and the fence (see the left middle photo).

Make the fence. To make a zero-clearance fence, cut a piece of scrap to the desired width and length. Depending on the size of your workpiece, this can vary from a full-length fence to a short piece that just covers the bit. Lower the bit below the surface of the table and attach the scrap fence to your existing fence. Attach this with clamps (as shown in the right middle photo), screws, or double-sided carpet tape. Then position the fence the desired distance away from the bit. Turn on the router and slowly raise the bit so it cuts into the auxiliary fence, stopping at the desired height. The simplest way to do this is to mark the final bit height on the scrap fence before raising the bit.

Using the fence. To use the fence, simply guide the workpiece past the bit. For small pieces, make sure to use one or more push blocks to keep your fingers away from the spinning bit (see the bottom photo).

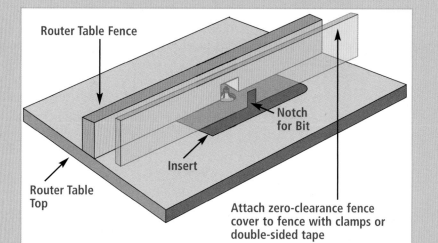

Router Table Fence

Notch for Bit

Insert

Router Table Top

Attach zero-clearance fence cover to fence with clamps or double-sided tape

Routing Small Pieces

When injuries occur with table-mounted routers, the common factor is often routing small pieces. There are two reasons for this, both a result of the size of the workpiece: There's little area to grip the workpiece securely, and fingers can and do get very near the spinning bit. The result of this combination can be a dangerous situation. The solution to both problems is to grip the workpiece with something other than your hands.

Use a grout float

A grout float is a great way to hold a small piece. The rubber face of the float will conform to the shape of the workpiece and hold it firmly (top photo). The large handle of the float provides excellent control while keeping your fingers far away from the bit.

Use a push block

If you don't have a grout float handy, use a push block. Push blocks can be store-bought (middle photo), or you can make one by simply notching a scrap of wood. Make sure to press firmly down on the workpiece with the push block as you guide it safely past the bit.

Use a clamp

Another method that works well for holding small pieces — especially very small pieces — is to clamp the workpiece between the jaws of a wood clamp, as shown in the bottom photo. Make sure to use only wood clamps, as a spinning bit hitting a metal clamp can ruin the workpiece, the bit, and your day.

Routing Grooves

Whether it's decorative or part of a joint, a groove can be cut accurately and quickly on a table-mounted router. Grooves are cut in the same direction as the wood grain of the workpiece. They are often cut with the workpiece on edge to accept a tongue or stub tenon to form either a tongue-and-groove joint or a stub-tenon-and-groove joint. Grooves are usually cut with a straight bit, but a spiral-end mill bit works well, particularly in woods with squirrelly grain, like bird's-eye maple, and other difficult-to-machine woods.

Position the fence

To cut a groove, first position the fence. Raise the bit above the table surface, and then position the fence so it's roughly the desired distance from the bit. Lock down one end of the fence and then use a metal rule to fine-tune the fence's position (top right photo). Pivot the fence as needed and then lock the loose end in place. If you need to make a centered groove, check out the sidebar on the opposite page.

Check the bit height

Next, check to make sure the bit will be able to make the cut to the full depth. Mark the workpiece and raise the bit to the mark (middle photo). If it doesn't reach, get a longer bit, or pull the bit out of the collet slightly. Remember, the collet should grip at least three-fourths of the bit's shank.

Rout the first pass

Once you're sure the bit can handle the groove you need to cut, readjust the bit height to cut about one-third of the finished depth. Multiple, light passes will create a cleaner groove while taxing the motor less. Press the workpiece firmly against the fence and feed it into the router from right to left (bottom photo).

Rout the second pass

After you've made your first pass, turn off the router and reset the bit height to make the second pass. The general rule of thumb is to make a cut in three or four passes, with the last being a very light clean-up pass (see below). Turn on the router and make the second pass, taking care to position the same face or edge of the workpiece against the router fence. Tip: Make an "X" on the face or edge of the workpiece that butts up against the fence so you won't forget and end up with a wider or misplaced groove.

Take a clean-up pass

In cases where a groove will be visible or needs to be extra-smooth, for example in a groove cut to accept a miter gauge, consider taking a final, very light clean-up pass to remove any torn wood fibers (middle photo). Often this can be done without adjusting the bit height. Just take another pass, pressing the workpiece hard into the bit. Alternatively, raise the bit just a hair and take another pass.

CENTERING A GROOVE

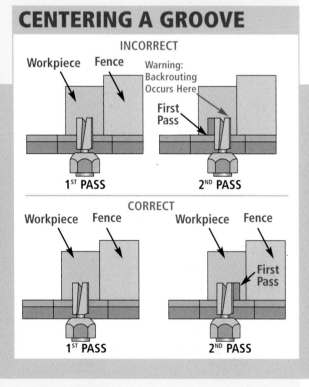

INCORRECT

Workpiece   Fence   Warning: Backrouting Occurs Here

First Pass

1ST PASS   2ND PASS

CORRECT

Workpiece   Fence   Workpiece   Fence

First Pass

1ST PASS   2ND PASS

SELF-CENTERING GROOVES

Many woodworkers spend considerable time tweaking the position of a router fence so that it'll make a true centered cut with a non-piloted bit, such as a straight bit used to rout a groove or mortise. The easiest way to get a perfectly centered cut is to use a narrower straight bit (for instance, use a ¼" bit to make a ⅜" groove) and take two passes, flipping the workpiece end-for-end between cuts. This perfectly centers the groove, and all you have to do is make a couple of test cuts, adjusting the fence, to get the proper width.

Routing Dadoes

Dadoes are U-shaped notches cut against the grain of a workpiece. Like grooves (pages 96–97), they're usually cut with a straight bit. But the cutting flutes of a spiral-end mill bit are angled, so you can often get a cleaner dado with one of these as they produce more of a shearing action on the cross-grain wood fibers.

Set the fence and bit

To rout a dado, begin by raising the bit above the table surface. Then roughly position the fence the desired distance from the bit (top photo). Lock down one end of the fence and pivot the other end until a metal rule indicates the final position; lock down the loose end of the fence. Next, lower the bit so it'll take about a one-third final depth cut, and lock it in place.

Rout the first pass

Turn on the router and, while pressing the workpiece firmly against the fence, guide it past the bit (middle photo). *Safety note:* Make sure to keep your hands away from the path of the bit, particularly where it exits the workpiece. Better yet, use a backer board (see the sidebar below).

PREVENTING CHIP-OUT WITH BACKER BOARD

When a straight bit or spiral-end mill bit exits a workpiece, there's no wood to support the wood fibers on the edge, so tear-out or chip-out will occur. To prevent this, support the wood fibers with a backer board — just a scrap of wood. Not only will this prevent tear-out, but it will also protect your hands if you get into the habit of stopping the cut shortly after the bit exits the workpiece and cuts into the backer board. Just pull the backer board away from the bit once it's free of the workpiece, and your fingers will be safe.

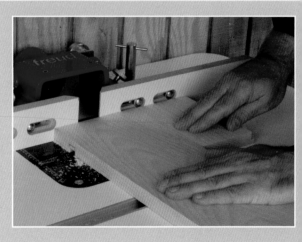

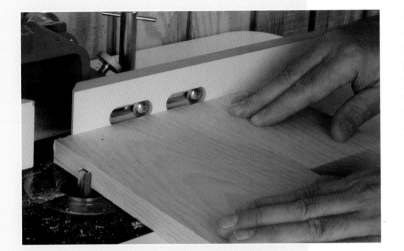

Rout the second pass

After taking the first pass, turn off the router and raise the bit for a second pass. Turn on the router and make the pass, using a backer board to prevent chip-out (see the photo at left). Repeat this procedure until the final depth of the dado is reached.

CLEAN-CUT DADOES

Because dadoes are cut against the grain, there's a significant risk of tear-out. In addition to using a spiral-end mill bit as described on page 98, consider using one or both of the following tricks.

Score first with a knife. One way to prevent tear-out when cutting dadoes is to sever the wood fibers in advance — this way they can't tear-out. Start by laying out the dado on your workpiece. Then, using a metal straightedge and sharp knife, cut cleanly along the marked line, see the upper photo at right. Cutting about 1/16" deep will suffice, as it's the surface fibers that have the greatest tendency to tear-out. Make sure to cut both marked lines.

Take a very light first pass. If you don't want to mess around with knife cuts, try taking an ultra-light first pass (lower photo). Set up the cut as you would normally, but adjust the bit height for a very light first pass — about 1/16" or less will do. Then turn on the router and make the pass; check out the router in the lower photo. This is similar to cutting with a knife, except you're also removing the waste between the sides of the dado. Now you can set the router for a deeper cut and proceed, taking three passes.

Rabbets

A rabbet is an L-shaped notch that's cut into the end or edge of a part. The notch is usually sized to accept another part. This offers a better gluing surface than the butt joint and also serves to lock the pieces together during assembly. But like the butt joint, a rabbet joint needs to be reinforced with fasteners to have any mechanical strength.

Rabbeting with a straight bit and fence

Although you can rout a rabbet using a rabbeting bit, rabbeting bits come only in incremental sizes. Because of this, many woodworkers use a straight bit and a fence to rout almost any size rabbet they need. To do this, start by selecting a straight bit with a diameter that's greater than the width of the rabbet you need to cut. Raise the bit above the table and then position the fence to cut the desired width (see the top right photo).

Take the first pass

With the fence set, lower the bit so it's about one-third the final depth of the rabbet. Turn on the router and, while pressing the workpiece firmly against the fence, slide the workpiece into the spinning bit (middle photo).

Make multiple passes

Turn off the router and raise the bit for the next pass. Flip the power on and make a pass (see the photo at right). Repeat until the final rabbet depth is reached.

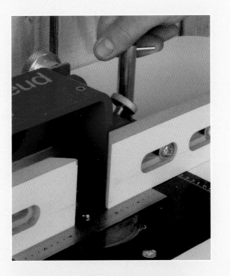

Rabbeting bit setup

Although you can rout a rabbet with a rabbeting bit without using a fence, you'll be better off if you use one. The reason is that the bearing of the rabbeting bit will inevitably leave a slight recess in the edge of the wood, called a bearing track. To make a full-width cut using a rabbeting bit, position the fence so it's flush with the bearing. The simplest way to do this is to place a metal rule across the bit opening, as shown in the photo at left, and adjust the fence until the rule just touches the bearing. This will completely eliminate bearing tracks. You can also rout rabbets that are narrower than the width of the rabbeting bit by simply positioning the fence for a narrower cut.

Routing with rabbeting bit

With the fence set, you can rout the rabbet as you would with a straight bit and a fence (middle photo on the opposite page). Just be sure to take multiple passes. Also, to prevent tear-out, consider taking a light first pass, as shown in the photo at left.

BACKROUTING TO PREVENT CHIP-OUT

Rabbeting bits have a well-deserved reputation for causing tear-out along the edge of a workpiece. That's because as the bit exits the workpiece, there's no wood to support the fibers at the edge. One way to prevent tear-out with a rabbeting bit is to take a very light first pass by feeding the workpiece in the opposite direction — commonly called backrouting. This should be done only on pieces that are long and wide, where there's little chance of your hands being pulled into the bit. Do not attempt this unless you have considerable experience with your table-mounted router — and even then be careful to take a light, skipping cut.

Routing Mortises

In some ways, routing mortises on a table-mounted router is more complicated than routing them with a handheld router. That's because you need to lower the workpiece onto the bit — even if the router is a plunge router. And in order to precisely locate the start and stop points of the mortise, you'll need to add stops (though technically, this isn't absolutely necessary). Although this may sound complicated, it's a fairly straightforward setup and seems simpler the more you do it. On the plus side, it's a whole lot easier to rout an offset mortise in a table-mounted router — all you have to do to offset the mortise is reposition the fence. That's something you can't easily do with a handheld router.

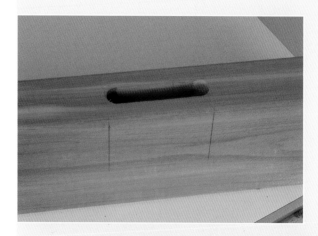

Lay out the mortise
The first step to routing a mortise on a table-mounted router is to lay out the location of the mortise on the workpiece. Then transfer marks that define the ends of the mortise to the side of the workpiece with a pencil and a try square, as shown in the middle photo at right. You'll use these marks later either to visually start and stop the cut or to add stops on the fence to serve as limits of the mortise. See the sidebar on page 105 for more on using stops.

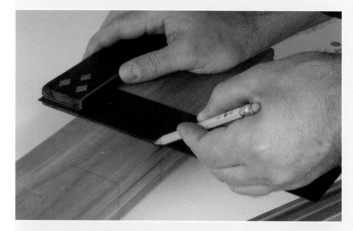

SPIRAL-END MILL BITS

Spiral-end mill bits (often simply called spiral bits) are specifically designed for cutting mortises (left bit in the photo at right). There are two basic designs: up spiral and down spiral. The direction refers to which way chips are ejected. Up spiral bits are best used when chip removal is a concern. Unlike standard straight bits, up spiral bits pull the chips out of the hole or mortise as they're being cut, similarly to the way the flutes on a twist bit operate. Down spiral bits are used when there are no chip removal issues. Both types feature angled flutes (usually two), which provide a shearing action that makes a much cleaner cut than a straight bit.

Set the bit and the fence

With the mortise marked, you can set up the bit and position the fence. Start by raising the bit above the surface of the table. Then butt the workpiece up against the bit as shown, and slide the fence over to butt up against the workpiece (top photo). Tweak the position of the fence as necessary to achieve the desired cut. Then adjust the bit to make a cut one-third to one-fourth the desired depth of the mortise.

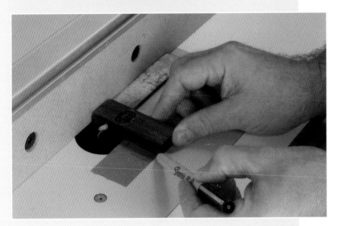

Mark bit location on tabletop

In order to align the marks you made earlier on your workpiece with the bit, you'll need to make marks on the tabletop, since the workpiece will obscure the bit during the cut. To do this, temporarily attach a strip of tape in front of the bit (instead of marking the top itself), and butt a try square up against the fence on both sides of the bit. Mark the tape on each side, as shown in the photo at left, in order to identify the location of the bit.

Align the marks

As we mentioned previously, you can rout a mortise with stops. This is fine for one or two mortises, but if you're routing a lot — or you want to guarantee that they start and stop at the right point — use stops (see page 105 for more on this). To rout a mortise without stops, turn on the router and hold the workpiece above the router, as shown, taking care to align the start of the mortise with the end of the bit.

Lower the workpiece to cut

Now all you have to do is slowly lower the workpiece down onto the bit. The only thing to keep in mind here is that you need to keep the face of the workpiece pressed firmly up against the fence to prevent routing an uneven mortise. Here, an up mill bit will come in extra-handy (see the sidebar on page 102), as the bit will pull chips out of the hole and make a clean cut.

Push workpiece to the other end

As soon as the workpiece bottoms out on the tabletop, start pushing the workpiece from right to left. Make sure you keep the face of the workpiece pressed up firmly against the fence (middle photo). It's important that you start moving immediately to prevent burning.

Lift up to clear the bit

As you reach the end of the mortise, slow down and then stop when the bit mark on the tabletop aligns with the end of the mortise mark on the workpiece. Now carefully raise the workpiece up off the bit (bottom photo). Although it would be best to lift the workpiece straight up, this doesn't offer any control. That's why most woodworkers lift up just the rear end while keeping the front of the workpiece on the tabletop. Once the workpiece has cleared the bit, turn off the router and raise the bit, repeating as necessary until the full mortise depth is reached.

USING STOPS

A stopped or partial cut is a common task that a table-mounted router is particularly well suited for — especially when routing mortises. Once your bit height and fence are set, all you need to do is clamp stops to the fence to limit the cut by defining the starting and stopping points.

Align marks with fence. To position a stop, make a pencil mark on your router table that defines the edge of the bit, as described on page 103. Then if you haven't already, mark the side of the workpiece where you want the mortise to start and stop. Now with the bit lowered beneath the table surface, place the workpiece against the fence so the marked end of the bit aligns with the starting point of the mortise as shown in the photo at top right.

Position the stop blocks. Now all you have to do is clamp a scrap of wood to the fence so it butts up against the end of the workpiece as shown in the middle photo. Repeat this procedure to identify the end of the mortise.

Rout the mortise. The mortise is routed by butting one end of the workpiece against one stop, lowering it onto the spinning bit, and then pushing it forward until it hits the other stop. The only difference here is that you won't be able to pivot the workpiece as described on the opposite page to lift the workpiece off the bit — the stop will prevent it from pivoting. Instead, you'll need to lift it straight up. The good thing is, now you have the stop to use as a guide to keep the workpiece straight.

SQUARING MORTISES

Mortises cut with a router have rounded ends to match the diameter of the bit. In some cases, such as when you need through mortises that are exposed, you may want to square up the ends of the mortise to accept a square tenon instead of rounding over the tenon as described on page 109.

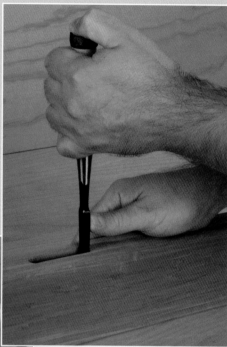

Freehand with a chisel. You can square the corners of a mortise with a bevel edge, a firmer, or a mortising chisel. Regardless of the type used, the edge must be razor-sharp to cleanly cut through the end grain. Hand pressure alone will work, as long as you use a firm grip and take light paring cuts, as shown in the photo at right. Just make sure to keep the chisel perfectly vertical.

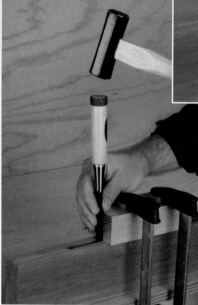

Adding precision with guide blocks. Keeping a chisel perfectly vertical when squaring a mortise is a difficult task. That's because the chisel will tend to follow the grain and will want to dig into the end grain instead of cutting it. A simple way to keep the chisel aligned is to clamp a square scrap block to the workpiece to serve as a guide; see the middle photo at right.

Using a corner chisel. A corner chisel is a special chisel that has two cutting edges that meet at a perfect 90-degree angle. Corner chisels are used to square up the corners of a mortise after most of the waste has been removed. The key to using a corner chisel effectively is to take only light, paring cuts and make sure to hold the chisel perfectly vertical. To help guide the chisel in straight, clamp a square scrap block to the workpiece. Stop often and clean out the waste. If you're cutting a through mortise, cut just halfway, flip the workpiece, and continue in from the other side.

Tenons

The part that mates with a mortise is a tenon, shown in the photo at right. The tenon may be square (as shown here) or rounded, as on page 109. Cutting a tenon on a table-mounted router is quick and easy, especially if your tabletop will accept a miter gauge. The length of the tenon is set by positioning the fence the desired distance from the bit. The tenon thickness is determined by the bit height.

Set the fence as a stop

To rout a tenon, start by inserting a straight bit into the router and raising the bit slightly above the tabletop. Then roughly position the fence the desired distance from the bit. Note that this is one case where it's important that the fence be parallel to the miter gauge slot. If it isn't, you'll cut a tapered tenon. The simplest way to make sure the fence is aligned with the miter gauge is to place one leg of a try square or framing square against the head of the miter gauge and butt the other leg up against the fence (see the photo at left). Adjust the fence so it's perpendicular to the miter gauge and set the correct distance from the bit.

Use a miter gauge and backer block

The best way to set the bit height is to roughly position the bit and then make a test cut, flipping the piece over to cut both sides to create a short tenon. Just be sure that the scrap piece you're making the test cut on is the exact thickness of the stock you'll be routing. All you need do is rout just about 1/4" off the end of the scrap so you can measure the thickness of the tenon. Whenever possible, test the fit by inserting the tenon in the mortise. To prevent tearout as the bit exits the workpiece, support the wood by slipping a backer block between the workpiece and miter gauge, as shown in the photo at left.

Work toward the fence

Once the bit height has been set and you're satisfied with the fit of the tenon in the mortise, you can switch to your good stock and start routing. Begin cutting the tenon by routing at the very end of the workpiece (top photo). Make a pass and then slide the workpiece away from the bit; pull the miter gauge back to the starting position. Slide the workpiece in so the end is a little closer to the fence, and make another pass.

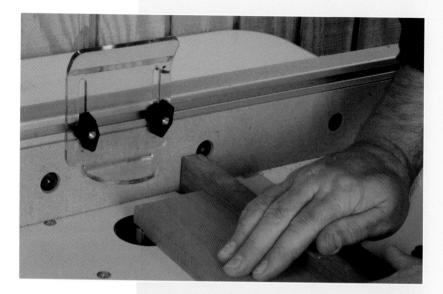

Take final pass

Continue routing and sliding the workpiece in toward the fence until the end of the workpiece contacts the fence (see the photo at right). This will be the final pass that defines the shoulder of the tenon. Because this shoulder will be highly visible, make a very light final pass and take it a little slower. This combination of a light pass and slower feed rate will help prevent tear-out on the face of the workpiece.

Flip and repeat

Once you've completed routing one cheek of the tenon, flip it over and repeat this process for the other cheek (bottom photo). If the tenon is to have four shoulders, flip the workpiece on edge and repeat the process for both shoulders. Depending on the width of the workpiece and the width of the tenon, the shoulder cuts may need to be deeper or shallower than the cheek cuts. If this is the case, cut the cheeks on all your pieces first, then reset the bit height and cut the shoulders on edge. This way all the tenons will be the same thickness.

ROUNDING TENONS

If you've cut your mortises with a router, the ends will be rounded to match the diameter of the router bit. When you rout a tenon, the ends are square. This creates the proverbial "square peg in a round hole" scenario. Either the ends of the mortise will need to be squared or the ends of the tenons will need to be rounded. Which you do is a matter of personal preference. In cases where the mortise is stopped (that is, it doesn't pass all the way through the workpiece), it's often easier to round the tenons. For techniques for squaring mortises, see page 106. There are two basic tools you can use to round over a tenon: a chisel and a rasp.

Paring with a chisel. Paring the ends of a tenon with a chisel can be done with a few quick cuts, as long as you've got a steady hand. How easy or difficult this is will depend a lot on the wood. Hardwoods with squirrelly grain can be challenging, as the chisel will tend to follow the grain and produce wandering cuts. Hardwoods and softwoods with straight grain are easier to cut, but can often split off more wood than you want to remove. The secret is to take lighter, paring cuts and make sure to clamp the workpiece to keep it from shifting as you cut (see the photo at left).

Four-in-hand rasp. A four-in-hand rasp (originally called a shoe rasp) is the perfect tool for rounding tenons, see the photo at left. It combines four tools in one, as it's double-ended and has a half-round shape. One end is a rasp, the other a file. Effectively, you have a half-round file, a flat file, a half-round rasp, and a flat rasp. What's great about this tool is that both edges are "safe" or smooth. This makes the four-in-hand rasp particularly useful when rounding over tenons because the tool will stop cutting when it hits the shoulder of the tenon.

Cleaning up shoulders. The only catch to using a four-in-hand rasp to round over tenons is that the rasp can't cut into the very corners of the tenon where it meets the shoulders. That's because the edges of the tool are smooth and the tool bottoms out when the edges hit the corners. Although this is good because you can't damage the shoulders, it does leave a small wedge of waste that will need to be removed with a sharp chisel (bottom photo). This is a small price to pay for protecting the shoulders from damage.

FINE-TUNING MORTISE-AND-TENON JOINTS

Since it's always better to have a tenon that's too big than too small (if it's too small, you'll need to recut it or fix it; see below), the tenon will often require a little paring to fit snugly. A wide chisel can make quick work of this when used with an underhand grip to lightly pare away the excess. Start at one end and use the lip created by the chisel to reference the next cut. Take light cuts and check the fit often. Alternatively, if you've got a shoulder plane in your tool chest, this works just as well as the chisel, if not better.

Relieving tenon shoulders. Once the tenon fits into the mortise, all that's left is to make sure the joint fits snugly together with no gaps. Even when you're careful cutting a tenon, it's easy to end up with a "stepped" shoulder. To clean up the shoulders, start by taking light, horizontal paring strokes to clean out the intersection of the cheek and shoulder. Another valuable technique is to undercut the shoulders. That is, instead of making a 90-degree cut, start just inside the shoulder (around 1/16") and tilt the chisel up slightly (top photo). This undercuts the shoulder and virtually eliminates any fitting problems.

Chamfering tenon ends. You can also relieve the ends of the tenon by chamfering them slightly (middle photo). This makes it easier to slide a tenon into a mortise, especially if the piece is complex and you're sliding multiple mortise-and-tenon joints together at the same time. You can chamfer the ends with a chisel (as shown), with a file, or with a block plane.

Loose tenon fix. If you find that your tenon is too loose in the mortise, here's a quick fix that will create a tight fit. Start by cutting a thin scrap of wood to the required thickness. Then glue this scrap to the tenon, taking care to align the wood grain as shown. After the glue dries, trim the scrap to width and length as necessary. If needed, pare or sand the scrap so the tenon fits snug in the mortise. If a very thin scrap is needed, consider using a wide shaving from a hand plane.

Loose Tenons

An interesting alternative to the mortise-and-tenon joint is a mortise-and-loose-tenon joint (top right photo). With this joint, mortises are cut in each of the pieces to be joined and a separate "loose" tenon is cut to join them together. Since most mortise-and-tenon joints are used to join cabinet pieces together (typically a vertical stile and a horizontal rail), routing one of the mortises can be tricky.

The mortise in the vertical stile can be routed like a standard mortise. But the mortise in the end of the horizontal rail can be challenging. The best way to do this is to use a router installed in a horizontal mortising jig (see page 45). With the horizontal mortising jig, the rail is laid flat on the table and the end is slid into the bit with the aid of a miter gauge. With a standard table-mounted router, you'd have to hold the rail vertically against the fence and lower it onto the bit — tough to do with any precision.

Rounding over ends

Once you've cut your mortises, all you need to do is make the loose tenons. Start by ripping or planing stock to thickness to fit in the mortises. Note that grain direction is critical here. To provide any strength, the grain of the tenon must be oriented as shown in the photo at left. If the grain runs the other way, the tenon will easily split in half when pressure is applied. The quickest way to round over the edges of the loose tenon is to rout them round with a round-over bit; see the photo at left. Choose a bit that matches the radius of the mortises.

Cut tenons to length

All that's left is to cut the tenons to length to fit into the mortises. Measure each mortise and add them together. Then cut a tenon about $1/16$" less than this to allow room for glue. If desired, chamfer the ends slightly to make it easier to slide them into the mortises.

Lap Joints

Making a lap joint on a table-mounted router is even easier than routing a tenon. That's because you rout only one face of the work-piece instead of both faces as when routing a tenon. The method used to cut this joint is very similar to that used for routing a tenon (see pages 107–111). The only challenge is getting the two halves the correct thickness so that the faces end up flush (see the photo above).

repeating test cuts until the tenon just disappears. If the bit is originally set too high, you'll get no tenon and you'll need to lower the bit. This method of sneaking up on the final thickness is used by experienced woodworkers everywhere.

Set the fence as a stop

To rout a lap joint (a half-lap joint is shown here), start by setting the fence to define the length of each half-lap. Insert a straight bit in the router and raise it so it's just above the tabletop. Then roughly position the fence for the desired length of each half-lap. An easy way to do this is to lay out the half-lap on the workpiece and align the shoulder mark with the bit. Then slide the fence over until it butts up against the end of the workpiece. Before you lock the fence in position, check with a try square to make sure the miter gauge is perpendicular to the fence (see the middle photo above).

Set the bit height and test the fit

Once the fence is in position, raise the bit up and make a test cut. If what you're after is a true half-lap, where each cheek is the same thickness, there's a quick way to check for proper thickness. Make a first cut at the end of a piece of scrap the same thickness as your workpiece. Then flip the scrap over and rout the other face near the end. If the bit is too low, you'll end up with a thin tenon like the one shown in the photo at right. Continue raising the bit slightly and

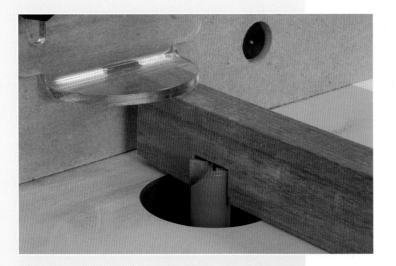

Prevent chip-out with a backer block

After you've got the bit set to the right height, you can rout your finished stock. Before you do, make sure to attach a temporary scrap of wood — a backer block — to the head of the miter gauge (see the photo at left). This scrap will prevent chip-out of the workpiece as the bit exits the trailing edge.

Rout the first half

Routing a half-lap uses the same technique as routing a tenon. Start by routing the end of the workpiece. Take a light pass and, when complete, slide the workpiece away from the bit and pull the miter gauge back to the starting position. Then slide the end of the workpiece closer to the bit and make another pass. Continue routing until the end of the workpiece butts up against the fence to define the shoulder of the joint (middle photo).

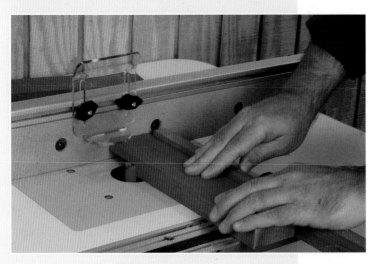

Rout the second half

With one-half of the joint done, you can rout the other half-lap using the method described above (bottom photo). Once you've finished the two halves of the joint, take the time to verify that the fit is perfect. Perfect here means that the faces of the workpieces end up flush with each other. If necessary, readjust bit height, and continue routing.

Box Joints

Box joints, often called finger joints, are an excellent way to join the sides of a box, case, or cabinet together (top photo). They're really handy for joining together thin stock, where other joints wouldn't provide sufficient gluing surface. The many fingers of a box joint provide excellent gluing surfaces to create a surprisingly strong joint. In the days before plastics and tin cans, many consumer goods came in wooden boxes, the sides of which were joined together with box joints — hence the name.

Cutting box joints on a table-mounted router requires a special box-joint jig to space or index the notches with precision, see the photo at right. You can purchase these (see page 45), or make one yourself. See pages 144–148 for step-by-step directions for a shop-made box-joint jig.

Set up the joint spacing
The trickiest part of using a box-joint jig is setting it up to cut accurately spaced notches in the workpieces. All box-joint jigs for a table-mounted router can only cut notches the size of commonly available straight bits, typically $1/8$", $1/4$", $3/8$", and $1/2$". This means you'll need to set the index pin of the box-joint jig away from the bit the same distance as its diameter. An easy way to do this is to use an equivalent-sized twist drill bit. Just insert the shank of the bit (a $1/4$" bit is shown here) between the index pin and the bit as a spacer (bottom photo). Then lock the box-joint jig in place (for more on the jig shown here, see pages 144–148). Even though this is a fairly accurate way to adjust the jig, you may have to tweak the position of the index pin after you've made a set of test cuts.

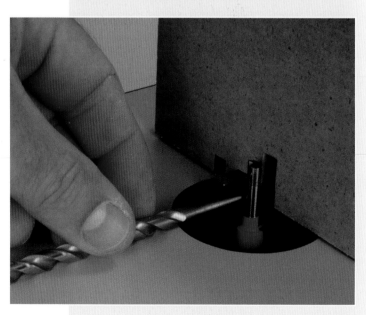

Set the bit height

With the jig set up, all that's left is to adjust the bit height. A simple way to do this is to use a piece of the stock as a guide. Just place a piece of stock face down on the tabletop and slide it over against the bit as shown in the photo at left. Raise or lower the bit so the end is flush with the face of the stock. Again, even though this is a relatively accurate way to set the bit, you may need to tweak its position after you've made test cuts.

Cut the first piece

To rout the notches in the first workpiece, set the piece on end against the miter gauge and slide it over until the edge butts up against the index pin. Then turn on the router and push the workpiece past the bit. There should be no problem with chip-out when the bit exits the workpiece since the jig will back up the cut. Remove the workpiece from the jig and slide it back to the starting position. Next, slip the notch you just cut over the index pin so the end is flat on the tabletop, and make a second pass (middle photo). Continue like this, lifting and moving the workpiece over until you've cut all the notches on the first piece.

Cut the mating piece

The piece that mates with the first must have its notches shifted over so they can accept the pins cut in the first piece. To do this, use the first piece as a spacer to locate the first notch in the mating piece (bottom photo). Make the first pass and then remove both pieces. Now slip the notch you cut in the mating piece over the index pin and continue cutting the notches as you did for the first piece. When complete, check the fit of the two parts. If they don't fit, increase the spacing between the index pin and the bit; if too loose, decrease the spacing. The pins should also be flush or slightly proud of the adjoining piece. If necessary, adjust bit height and make another set of test cuts — just make sure to always use scrap that's the same thickness as your workpiece stock.

Cope-and-Stick Joint

The cope-and-stick joint has been used for decades in industrial cabinet production — especially for making kitchen cabinet frame-and-panel doors. That's because the joint is very strong: It offers excellent gluing surfaces. It's also attractive, and it simplifies construction since it also cuts the groove for the panel at the same time as the joint. Cope-and-stick joints can be routed with separate bits — always sold as matched sets — or with a single, multipurpose bit as shown here. The stick half of the joint is usually routed along the length of the stiles of a frame; the cope half is routed on the ends of the rails and along the inside edge (see the drawing at right). Because cope-and-stick bits are large and they require the use of a miter gauge and fence (or a sled, see page 43), they should be cut only on a table-mounted router.

rout. Once the end is routed, rout the same profile along the inside edge. Note: Mark the ends of the rails and all the inside edges of your workpieces with an "X" to make sure you rout the right spot.

COPE-AND-STICK ANATOMY

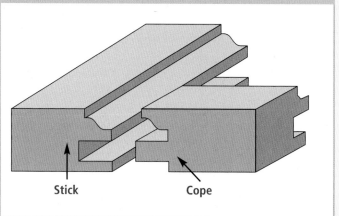

Stick   Cope

Set the bit and the fence
How you set up the bit and fence to rout a cope-and-stick joint depends on the bit set or bit you're using. Read and follow the manufacturer's directions carefully, as setting these up will take patience and some trial-and-error test cuts. Virtually all of these bits or bit sets use an internal bearing to set the width of cut. All you have to be concerned with is setting the bit to the correct height, see the upper photo at right.

Rout the cope
Once you have the bit height correct, you can rout one-half of the joint. In our case, we started with the cope. Use the miter gauge to slide the workpiece past the spinning bit. Insert a backer board between the workpiece and miter gauge to prevent chip-out (bottom photo). Cope-and-stick bits are one of the few types where it's best to make the cut in a single pass. Keep a firm grip on the workpiece and make sure the end contacts the internal bearing of the bit as you

Adjust bit for the stick cut

If you are using a multi-purpose bit to rout this joint as shown here, the next step is to adjust the bit to rout the stick. This is simply a matter of raising or lowering the bit following the manufacturer's directions (top photo).
If instead you're using a matched bit set, change bits to make the second profile and adjust the bit height as needed.

Rout the stick

With the bit adjusted, or with the matching bit in place, rout the mating half (middle photo). For the stick cut, you'll be routing along the inside edge of the workpiece. You'll be taking off a lot of material, so keep a firm grip and finish pushing the workpiece past the bit with a push stick to protect your fingers.

Test the fit

With both parts routed, you can test the fit (the bottom photo at left). Hopefully, they'll mate perfectly, with the faces absolutely flush. If they do, mark and keep these two pieces as master templates for setting up the bits for future use. The two parts will always fit together well because the bit profiles will ensure this. The tricky part is getting the faces of the workpieces flush. If they're not, you'll have to fiddle with bit height on one or both cuts. Realize that this will take some trial and error. But once you've got it and you've saved your templates, future setup will be a breeze.

Raised Panels

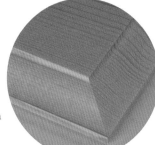

Cabinet doors, sides of chests, and cases are often made using frame-and-panel construction. The frame consists of vertical stiles and horizontal rails and are commonly joined with mortise-and-tenon or cope-and-stick joints. Grooves are cut along the inside edges to accept a panel that usually "floats" in the frame, letting it expand and contract as the seasons change. The panel is typically pinned to the rails in the center to keep it in position.

Panels can be plain flat pieces or have their edges molded in a variety of profiles. Profiling the edges does three things: It creates an attractive panel; it reduces the edge thickness so the panel can fit in the grooves of the frame; and it "raises" the center of the panel, creating a richer, more 3-D effect. Panel raising requires special bits. These are either horizontal or vertical (see pages 32–33). In both cases the bits are large and therefore should be used only on routers mounted in a table. Because horizontal panel-raising bits are so large and the outer rim speeds are dangerously fast, we prefer vertical panel-raising bits.

Add a tall fence
Because vertical panel-raising bits require you to rout the workpiece on its edge, it's imperative that you attach a tall auxiliary fence to your existing fence to provide stable support to the workpiece (see the middle photo at right). In most cases, the auxiliary fence is best attached to the router fence from behind with screws. This way there's nothing to interfere with the workpiece as it's moved past the bit. Alternatively, if you have a horizontal mortising jig for your router (see page 45), consider using this instead of a router table. You'll get the best of both worlds: You'll be able to lay the workpiece flat on the table so gravity works for you, and you can use a smaller, safer vertical panel-raising bit.

Rout the end grain first
Once the fence is in place, you can adjust the bit for the first of many passes. There are two ways to make multiple, light passes with one of these bits. One way is to slowly raise the bit up between passes until the full profile is achieved. The other method is to adjust the bit height for a full profile and then move the fence forward to take a light cut, easing it back to slowly expose more of the bit until the full profile is cut. Whichever method you choose, make sure to start routing the end grain first (bottom photo). This way if there's any tear-out, it'll be removed when you rout the edge grain.

Rout the edge grain

After you've routed both ends of the panel, rotate it to cut the edge grain (see the photo at top left). Make sure to press the workpiece firmly into the fence as you make each pass. If your tabletop has a miter gauge slot, consider using one of the many featherboards that fit in it. These featherboards can be adjusted to provide uniform, firm pressure while also preventing kickback.

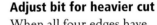

Adjust bit for heavier cut

When all four edges have been routed, adjust the bit or the fence for a heavier cut and repeat the process, routing the end grain first, followed by the edge grain (middle photo). For a standard profile in $3/4$" stock, you'll want to take five to six light passes to complete the profile. Remember: These bits have to remove a lot of wood, so it's safer for you and easier on the router and bit to do this slowly.

Make final light pass

The final pass you make should be the lightest. This way you'll reduce tear-out and splintering of the face grain — especially along the end of the panel, where the end grain is very susceptible to this. When you've completed your final pass, you may notice that the ends of the panel are a bit fuzzy. Remove any lifted fiber with fine sandpaper wrapped around a block (bottom photo). Make sure to sand *with* the grain to prevent cross-grain scratches.

Decorative Profiles

Routing decorative profiles on a table-mounted router is one of the simplest operations you can perform. That's because many decorative profile bits are piloted. These include round-over bits, chamfers, ogees, and beading bits. With these bits, all you have to do to create the profile is run the edge of the workpiece along the bearing-guided bit. Profile bits that are non-piloted, such as core-box bits, fluting bits, and others, will need the fence and/or a miter gauge to guide the workpiece.

Routing profiles on end grain

Routing a profile on the end of a workpiece can be tricky because you're cutting end grain (middle photo). There are two things to be aware of. First, the tougher end grain is more difficult for the router bit to cut cleanly, so it's important that the bit be sharp and that you take light cuts, working up to the desired profile. Second, as you end the cut, the chances of chip-out are huge, as the unsupported end grain is easy to splinter off. See the opposite page for ways of preventing this chip-out.

Routing profiles on edge grain

Profiles routed along the edge grain of a workpiece can be routed with the workpiece lying flat on the tabletop, or with the end edge pressed up against the fence as shown in the bottom photo. As always, the profile should be routed with a series of light passes to minimize chances of tear-out, along with reducing the strain on the router and the bit. The only real danger of chip-out will occur as the front edge of the workpiece is presented to the bit; for a number of ways to prevent this, see the opposite page.

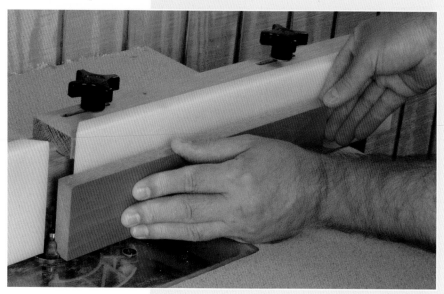

PREVENTING CHIP-OUT WITH DECORATIVE BITS

The last thing you want when routing a decorative profile is chip-out. That's because not only will the profile be highly visible, but it will often also be a surface that hands will touch — and a chip missing from the edge will be noticeable to both hand and eye. Here are three ways to prevent chip-out.

Use a backer board. Chip-out occurs when the router bit makes a cut and there is no wood to support the fibers being cut. On end grain, this is at the end of the cut; on edge grain, it's at the beginning of the cut. One way to keep chip-out from happening is to provide the needed support by placing a "sacrificial" scrap of wood — a backer block — behind the workpiece, as shown in the photo at right. This piece will still experience chip-out, but that's okay since it is scrap.

Consider backrouting. Another method that can be used sparingly to prevent chip-out is to make a light pass along the edge in the opposite direction of normal feed (middle photo). This is called backrouting and should be used only by experienced woodworkers who are used to their router and table. And, backrouting is only for larger workpieces that afford a good grip, where your fingers don't have any chance of contacting the bit. A firm grip is essential because backrouting will tend to grab the workpiece and pull it (and possibly your fingers) into the bit. By just scoring the edge, you'll remove the wood that's most likely to chip-out.

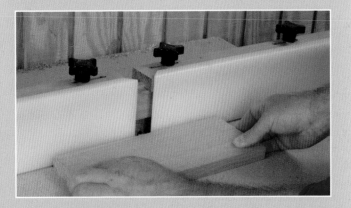

Rout the end grain first. The final method doesn't actually prevent chip-out — what it does is remove an edge where chip-out has already occurred. This technique is all about routing sequence. Start by routing the end grain of the workpiece first; chip-out will likely occur at the ends (bottom photo). Then rout the edge grain. In all but severe cases of chip-out, the edge grain pass will remove any visible chip-out.

Flutes

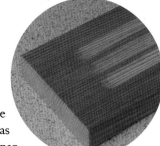

Flutes are a series of parallel grooves that are routed in a workpiece as decoration. They look particularly good on vertical trim pieces, such as columns on fireplace mantels, dividers on built-in bookcases, and several other classic furniture pieces. Although flutes are typically cut with a core-box bit (see page 30), they can also be cut with a V-groove bit (see page 30). The only trick to cutting these is spacing the grooves evenly. The easiest way to do this is with spacers, see below.

Set up the fence
To rout flutes in a workpiece, start by inserting a core-box or V-groove bit in the router and then raise it so the bit is above the tabletop. Then position the fence to rout the groove in the desired location. If you're using spacers to set the groove position, you may be able to use one (as shown here) to position the fence for the first cut.

Add the stops
If you're planning on routing stopped flutes instead of flutes that run the entire length of the workpiece, you'll need to add stops. Any scrap will do, if it's tall enough to clamp securely to the fence and wide enough to accommodate any spacers you may be using. Set your workpiece against the fence as shown (middle photo), and line up the bit with the ends of the flutes marked on the workpiece. Then slide a stop gently up against the end of the workpiece and clamp it in place. Repeat for the other end if necessary.

Lower to start the cut
With the stops in place, you can begin routing. Start by butting one end of the workpiece up against the stop, as shown in the bottom photo. Then gently lower the workpiece onto the spinning bit to start the cut.

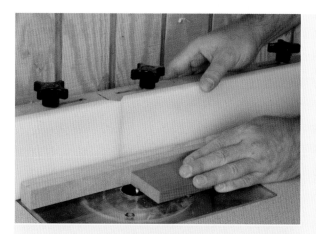

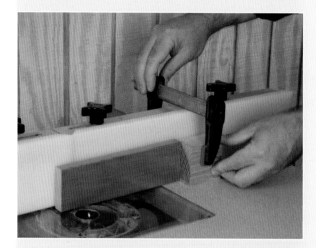

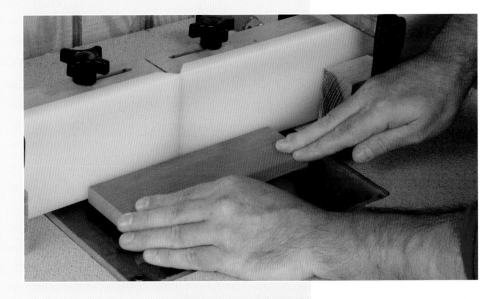

Push to other stop

As soon as the face of the workpiece bottoms out on the tabletop, start pushing it toward the opposite stop (top photo). This drop-and-push action really needs to be a single, fluid motion to prevent burning. With this in mind, it's worth taking the time to practice first on scrap wood until you've got the motion down pat.

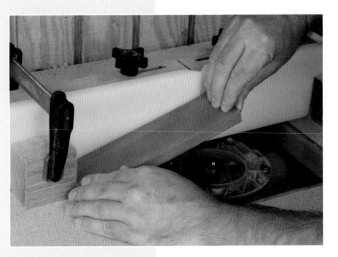

Lift to finish cut

Continue pushing the workpiece until the end butts up against the opposite stop block. You'll need to lift up the workpiece as soon as it hits the stop; otherwise, burning will occur (middle photo). Practice will help to make this motion fluid.

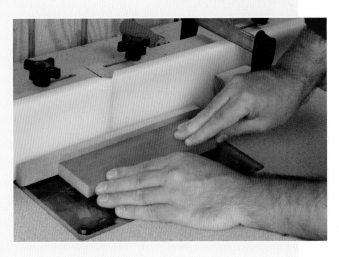

Add spacers for additional cuts

To rout the next parallel groove, add a spacer between the fence and the bit to move the cut over (bottom photo). If you're planning on a lot of parallel flutes, consider using a setup similar to the one for making the grooves in the trivet project featured on pages 187–189. The setup is shown on page 188. This system allows you to rout as many flutes as you want while ensuring that they're parallel.

■ SPECIAL TECHNIQUES

MAKING DOWELS

If you've ever built a project that called for dowels and you couldn't find any that matched the wood you were working with, you'll appreciate this technique for making your own dowels (see the photo at near right). Just think about it — dowels that perfectly match the rest of the project. No more sorting through dozens of dowels at the store trying to find a match (assuming you can even find a store that carries hardwood dowels in, say, maple, cherry, red and white oak, walnut, mahogany, etc.).

The only limitation to making your own dowels is that their finished diameters will depend on the incremental size of round-over bits available. This means you can make dowels that are the following diameters: $1/4$", $3/8$", $1/2$", $5/8$", $3/4$", 1", and up to $1^1/2$", all by using round-over bits that are $1/8$", $3/16$", $1/4$", $5/16$", $3/8$", $1/2$", and $3/4$", respectively (see the top photo at right).

Set up the bit. To make your own dowels, start by inserting the desired round-over bit in the router. Depending on the size of the dowel you'll be making, you may need to make multiple passes to achieve the full diameter. For bits that are $1/4$" diameter or less, you can make the profile in a single pass. With all other bits, you should take multiple light cuts, raising the bit after each pass.

Round over edges, leaving the ends square. The secret to making your own dowels is to leave the ends square (middle photo at right). This way you've got a flat reference surface that won't let the workpiece roll as you rout. Start each cut a couple of inches in from the end of the workpiece, and stop

routing an inch or two from the end. Then rotate the piece and rout again. Continue routing and rotating until the workpiece is round (see the routing sequence drawing at bottom).

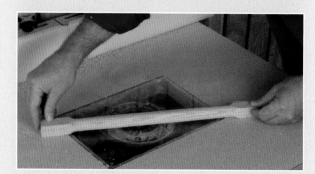

DOWEL-MAKING SEQUENCE

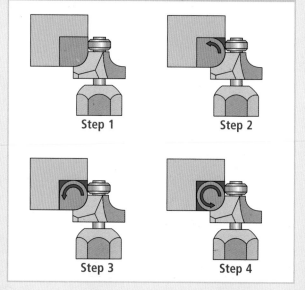

Step 1

Step 2

Step 3

Step 4

ROUNDING OVER DOWEL ENDS

Another special technique that's useful every now and then is rounding over the ends of a dowel. This is handy when making stools or any project that requires a nicely finished dowel. Many woodworkers would do this by hand-sanding, but this is tedious work, and it's hard to create a uniform round-over. A round-over bit will make quick work of this task. The only challenge is presenting the workpiece to the bit in a safe manner. For this we use an auxiliary fence, as discussed below.

Set the bit and fence. Insert the round-over bit of your choice, and raise the bit to the desired height. Then adjust the fence so that the faces are flush with the bearing on the round-over bit. A metal rule across the faces makes this easy to align, see the photo at top left.

Add the auxiliary fence. To rout the round-over, you want to present the dowel to the bit so the dowel is perfectly centered on the bit and rubs up against the bearing. This would be almost impossible to do freehand. That's why we clamp an auxiliary fence to the tabletop (middle photo). Position the fence so that the center of the dowel and the bit are aligned.

Rout and twist. Now you have a way to accurately and safely guide the dowel against the bit. Turn on the router and, with the dowel pressed up against the auxiliary fence, push the end of the dowel into the spinning bit. As soon as it bottoms out against the bearing, start rotating the dowel counterclockwise until the entire end is rounded over (bottom photo).

Jointing with a Router

Yes, the router is so versatile, you can even use it to joint wood (see the photo at right). The only limitation here is stock thickness. If you're using a standard straight bit, you'll be able to joint stock that's 3/4" thick or less.

Add laminate to the fence

Here's how it works. Attach a piece of plastic laminate to the outfeed side of your router table fence (see the top right photo). This effectively creates an infeed and an outfeed table just like a jointer (see the drawing below). This way, though, it's easier to handle large pieces since they lie flat on the router table instead of being held vertically, as with a jointer.

Set up the fence

Insert a straight bit into the router, preferably a 3/4" bit with a 3/4" shank — its stouter width will help prevent it from bowing under the cut. Adjust the fence so that the plastic laminate is flush with the edge of the bit, as shown in the drawing below.

Joint the edge

Once the bit and fence are set, you can joint the edge of your workpiece (bottom photo). Turn on the router and simply run the edge along the fence, making sure to transfer pressure to the outfeed side as the workpiece passes by the bit.

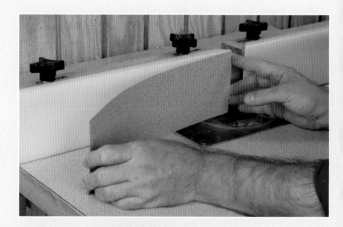

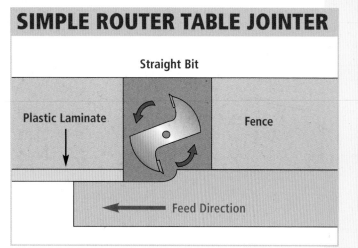

SIMPLE ROUTER TABLE JOINTER

Straight Bit

Plastic Laminate

Fence

Feed Direction

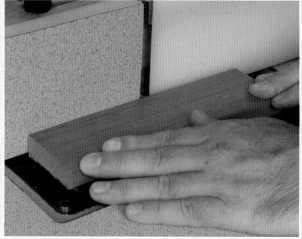

Using a Pin Arm

Attaching a pin arm to a table-mounted router turns the router into a duplicating machine. The pin arm is a simple device that holds a pin directly over the router bit (see the drawing below). By attaching a template to a workpiece, the pin can follow the template while the bit routs a matching pattern on the underside of the workpiece (see the photo at top left). For more on routing with a pin arm, see the desk clock project on pages 178–180.

Set up the arm

To set up the pin arm, position the pin so it's directly above the router bit (middle photo). Then clamp the body of the pin arm securely to the tabletop.

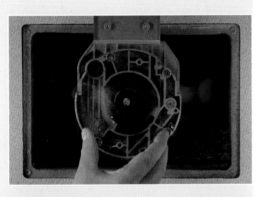

Rout the pattern

To use the pin arm, raise the arm and insert the workpiece with the pattern attached under the arm. Turn on the router and plunge the workpiece into the spinning bit. Tighten the knob on the top of the arm to keep the arm from rising up. Then make a series of light cuts until the pin butts up against the template attached to the workpiece (bottom photo).

Continue routing until all waste is removed. Then turn off the router, loosen the arm knob, and slide out the workpiece. If necessary, raise the bit and repeat until the desired depth is reached.

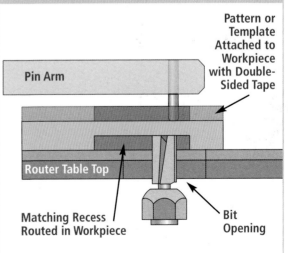

PIN-ARM ROUTER

Pattern or Template Attached to Workpiece with Double-Sided Tape

Pin Arm

Router Table Top

Matching Recess Routed in Workpiece

Bit Opening

5 Shop-Made Router Jigs & Fixtures

A router by itself is an amazingly versatile tool. When you start hooking it up to router jigs, though, the variety of tasks it can handle seems almost endless. A jig is any device that you attach to the router so it can do tricks. This chapter describes how to build and use seven jigs: for the portable router, a straightedge for accurately cutting grooves and dadoes, an oversized base plate to replace your original base plate, to make it easy to rout large recesses and generally give you better control of the router, and a circle jig for cutting precise circles.

There's a router bit cabinet to store and protect your collection of router bits. And for a table-mounted router, a box-joint jig for cutting box joints with ease. Speaking of router tables, they're the ultimate "jig" for a router. We've included plans to make your own table as well as an easy-to-use clamp-on fence with adjustable faces. Step-by-step instructions, an exploded view drawing, and a materials list make each of the jigs easy to make. Build one or all, and teach your router new tricks.

What's a router without jigs? A very versatile tool. What's a router with jigs? A tool that can handle almost any task in the shop. Shown here are just a few of the jigs described in this chapter.

Portable Router Straightedge

One of the most common routing tasks with a portable router is to make a straight cut, such as a groove or a dado in a workpiece. The usual options here are to use a relatively straight piece of wood for a guide and clamp it to the workpiece, or to use a low-profile clamp (see page 34). The problem with both of these is that there's no guarantee the router will remain in constant contact with the guide and that the router won't rotate. Both of these can cause inaccurate cuts. The straight-edge guide shown here eliminates both problems to ensure precise cuts.

The secret to this jig's accuracy comes from a pair of interlocking aluminum angle strips (see the Exploded View at right). A long strip attaches to a plywood guide strip; the shorter strip is secured to a sliding base that holds the router. Oversized holes in the short piece let you adjust the sliding base so it locks tightly into a matching channel in the guide strip, while still allowing for smooth travel.

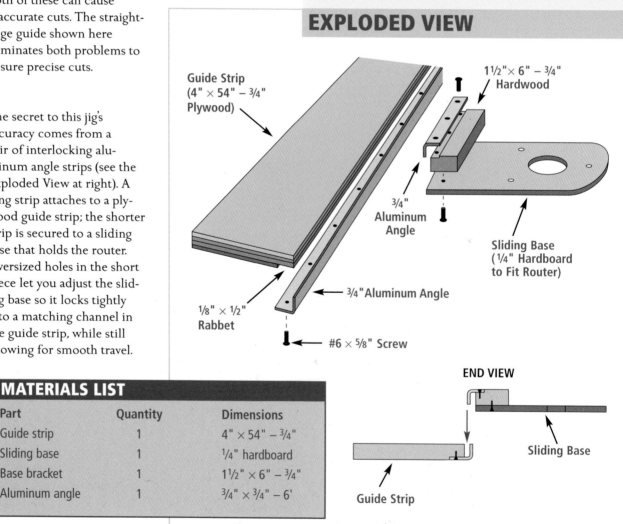

EXPLODED VIEW

Guide Strip (4" × 54" − 3/4" Plywood)

1 1/2" × 6" − 3/4" Hardwood

3/4" Aluminum Angle

Sliding Base (1/4" Hardboard to Fit Router)

1/8" × 1/2" Rabbet

3/4" Aluminum Angle

#6 × 5/8" Screw

END VIEW

Sliding Base

Guide Strip

MATERIALS LIST

Part	Quantity	Dimensions
Guide strip	1	4" × 54" − 3/4"
Sliding base	1	1/4" hardboard
Base bracket	1	1 1/2" × 6" − 3/4"
Aluminum angle	1	3/4" × 3/4" − 6'

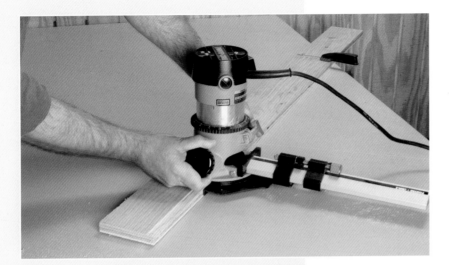

Rabbet the guide strip

To make the straightedge, begin by cutting the guide strip to width and length. Then rout a shallow rabbet along one edge to accept the aluminum angle, see the photo at left. For a $3/4" \times 3/4"$ angle, this rabbet is $1/8"$ deep and $1/2"$ wide. The idea is to create a $1/8"$ gap between the edge of the guide strip and the angle once it's attached. The angle on the base bracket will slip into this gap.

Attach the aluminum angle

Once the rabbet is cut, you can attach the aluminum angle to the guide strip (middle photo). To ensure you leave at least a $1/8"$ gap between the edge of the guide strip and the angle, insert a scrap piece of angle between the two when you screw it in place. Before you do this, you'll need to drill countersunk pilot holes in the bottom of the aluminum angle for the mounting screws. Start these 1" from each end of the angle and space them approximately 5" to 6" apart. Attach the angle with $\#6 \times 5/8"$ flathead woodscrews.

Make the base bracket

With the guide strip complete, you can turn your attention to the sliding base. The first part to make is the base bracket that accepts the short piece of aluminum angle. You'll need to rout a shallow rabbet ($1/8"$ deep and $1/2"$ wide) in the top edge for the angle. If you're doing this with a portable router, use an edge guide and place the bracket on a router pad (bottom photo). The bracket is $1^1/2"$ wide and cut to match the diameter of your router's base.

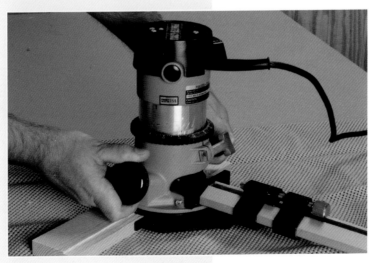

Make the router base

The sliding base is just a piece of $1/4$" hardboard cut to fit your router. It attaches to the base bracket with screws driven through the base and into the bracket. Cut the sliding base to width to match the diameter of your router and to sufficient length so the router base will not come in contact with the base bracket. Remove the plastic base plate of your router and use this to mark the bit opening and mounting holes (top photo). If desired, trace around the base and cut the end opposite the base bracket round. Drill the bit and mounting holes, and attach the sliding base to the bracket with $\#6 \times 5/8$" woodscrews. Drill the bracket mounting holes slightly oversized so you can adjust the gap for smooth operation before securing the angle to the bracket.

USING THE STRAIGHTEDGE

To use the straightedge, clamp it to your workpiece so that it's parallel to, and the desired distance from, the edge, as shown in the middle photo. If you mount your router to the sliding base so the knobs are oriented as shown in the bottom photo, you'll never have a problem with them running into the clamps, something that often happens with just a strip of wood used as a guide.

Now all that's left is to slide the base gently along the guide strip. This is best done on a scrap piece first to make sure that the base doesn't bind anywhere along the guide strip. If it does, or if it's too loose in places, inspect the gap between the aluminum angle and the guide strip. Loosen the screws and, if necessary, drill oversized holes in the strip so that you can adjust the position of the aluminum angle where it binds or is too loose.

Once the sliding base operates smoothly, you can make your cuts (see the bottom photo). As always, it's best to make your cut in a series of light passes (see page 53).

Oversized Base Plate

About as often as woodworkers wish for a third hand, most also wish the base plate on their router was just a little bit bigger. A larger base plate offers a more stable routing platform and is an absolute necessity when routing recesses like the one shown in the photo at left. A smaller base plate would simply dip into the recess and ruin the cut. The problem with many oversized base plates is that they're often made from an opaque material that makes seeing what you're cutting really difficult. To get around this common problem, we chose clear acrylic to make our base plate.

Increasing the size of the base plate also allows you to add an auxiliary knob for greater control. Once you start using one of these on your portable router, you're apt to leave it in place while the original plate collects dust on a shelf.

EXPLODED VIEW

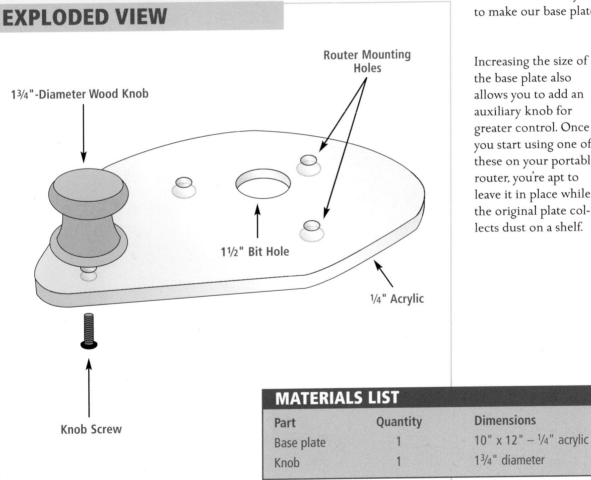

1¾"-Diameter Wood Knob

Router Mounting Holes

1½" Bit Hole

¼" Acrylic

Knob Screw

MATERIALS LIST

Part	Quantity	Dimensions
Base plate	1	10" x 12" – ¼" acrylic
Knob	1	1¾" diameter

Trace base on blank

There's really no limit to the size of the base plate you make for your router — it's really up to you. To make an oversized plate, start by placing your router's original base plate on a piece of clear acrylic. For a plate like the one shown here that's 2" larger around the perimeter, you'll need a piece of acrylic that's 10" wide and around 12" long. The easiest way to mark the plate is to use a scrap of wood with a hole drilled in it 2" from one edge. Then insert a permanent marker into the hole and trace around the base as shown in the photo at right. At the same time, mark the mounting hole locations and the bit opening.

Cut base to size

After you've marked the sheet of acrylic, you can cut the base plate to size. To do this, use a coping saw, a saber saw, or as shown in the middle photo, a band saw. When cutting plastic, it's important to move the blade through the workpiece, or the workpiece past the blade, at a steady clip. If you hesitate at all, the friction created by the blade will actually heat the plastic to the melting point and create an awful mess.

Drill holes

With the plate cut to size, you can drill the mounting holes, bit opening, and knob-screw hole. Countersink

the bottom of the mounting holes for the screws that attach the router to the plate. A hole saw works best for cutting the bit opening (bottom right photo); drill halfway through both sides for the cleanest hole.

FLAME-TREATING PLASTIC EDGES

The sawn edges of the acrylic base plate will be rough and show saw marks. These are easy to remove by flame-treating the edges. In effect, all you're doing is melting the plastic edge enough to melt the ridges so it flows to create a smooth edge. A propane torch commonly used to sweat pipe works great for this. Make sure to direct the flame only at the edges, and keep it moving to prevent the plastic from catching fire.

Add the auxiliary knob

To complete the oversized base plate, add the auxiliary control knob (top photo). Pick one that fits nicely in the palm of your hand. A 1³/₄"- to 2"-diameter knob will work for most folks. You'll need to countersink the bottom of its mounting hole to prevent the knob screw from catching on a workpiece. This is an option, and if you don't think it's necessary, skip this step. Odds are, though, that you'll find that an extra knob gives you better control of your router.

USING THE BASE PLATE

To use the oversized base plate, first attach it to your router. Place your router upside down on a work surface and position the base plate onto the sub-base so the mounting holes in the plate align with the threaded holes in the sub-base. Then thread in the mounting screws and drive them down until they're friction-tight. Then tighten them fully, alternating from screw to screw to prevent the plate from twisting or warping as the screws are tightened, as shown in the photo at bottom right.

Now you can insert a bit in the router, adjust it for the desired depth of cut, and rout away (see the photo below). Not only will the router be easier to handle, but you'll also be able to clearly see what you're routing.

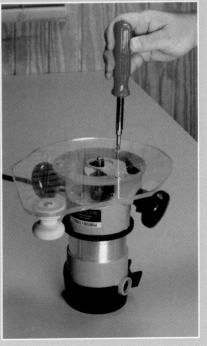

Circle-Cutting Jig

The router is the ultimate tool for cutting circles in wood. That's because it cuts such a clean edge, no sanding is required, unlike cutting with a saber saw or coping saw. And if you use a jig to guide the cut, the circle will be perfectly round. The problem with most circle jigs is that they usually have to be attached directly to the workpiece so they can pivot in a circle. Additionally, they're often difficult or impossible to adjust. Most of the time this is a trial-and-error guessing game.

Adjustments are no problem with the circle jig shown here: It's 100% adjustable. You can move and tweak the final position of the router bit with ease because the base plate that holds the router connects to a pivot block via a threaded rod and a pair of wing nuts. And thanks to a separate pivot base that's secured to the workpiece with double-sided carpet tape, you don't have to mar your workpiece. What's really nice about the pivot base and pivot block arrangement is that the pivot pin inserts into a plastic spacer that's set into the underside of the pivot block. This setup provides smooth pivoting action, which results in clean, precise circles every time. Note: To rout small circles, see the small circle base plate on page 139.

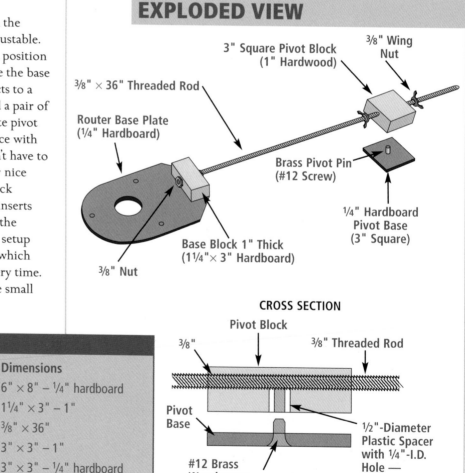

EXPLODED VIEW

3" Square Pivot Block
(1" Hardwood)

3/8" Wing Nut

3/8" × 36" Threaded Rod

Router Base Plate
(1/4" Hardboard)

Brass Pivot Pin
(#12 Screw)

1/4" Hardboard
Pivot Base
(3" Square)

Base Block 1" Thick
(1 1/4" × 3" Hardboard)

3/8" Nut

CROSS SECTION

Pivot Block

3/8"

3/8" Threaded Rod

Pivot Base

#12 Brass
Woodscrew
Cut 5/8" Long

1/2"-Diameter
Plastic Spacer
with 1/4"-I.D.
Hole —
1/2" Long

MATERIALS LIST

Part	Quantity	Dimensions
Base plate	1	6" × 8" – 1/4" hardboard
Base block	1	1 1/4" × 3" – 1"
Threaded rod	1	3/8" × 36"
Pivot block	1	3" × 3" – 1"
Pivot base	1	3" × 3" – 1/4" hardboard

Drill rod holes

The threaded rod that's the heart of this circle jig connects to the pivot and router base via a pivot and base block. To allow clearance for the plastic spacer installed in the pivot block, the holes for the threaded rod are $5/16$" down from the top edge of each block and centered on the width of each block. Drill these $3/8$"-diameter holes completely through each block. The best tool for this is the drill press, but you can use a portable drill, as long as you're careful to hold the drill perfectly vertical.

Pivot block and base

Next, drill the hole in the underside of the pivot block for the plastic spacer that will eventually fit over the pin on the pivot block (right photo). You can use any outside diameter plastic spacer as long as the inner diameter is $1/4$". We used a $1/2$"-long spacer with a $1/2$" outer diameter. This hole is $1/2$" deep, centered in the block. The pivot base is just a square of $1/4$" hardboard with a cut-off #12 woodscrew in the center. Cut the screw to a length of $5/8$", file a slight chamfer on the end, and epoxy it to the base (the Cross Section on the opposite page).

Base assembly

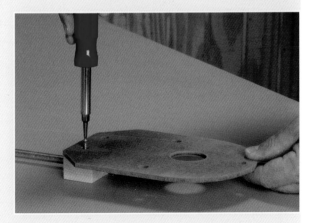

The base assembly consists of the base block attached to a $1/4$" hardboard plate that accepts your router. For a fixed-base router with a 6"-diameter base, the plate is 6" × 8". Use the original base plate to mark the mounting hole locations and bit opening. After you've drilled these and countersunk the mounting holes, attach the base block to the base plate with #8 × $3/4$" flathead woodscrews and glue. Then insert the threaded rod into the base block and pivot block. Secure it to the base block with a pair of $3/8$" nuts and to the pivot block with two $3/8$" wing nuts.

USING THE CIRCLE JIG

To use the circle jig, start by attaching the pivot base to your workpiece. Find the exact center of the workpiece and draw a pair of perpendicular lines. Then align the corners of the pivot base with the marked lines and secure it to the workpiece with a couple of strips of double-sided carpet tape. Warning: Make sure to slip a scrap of plywood under your workpiece if you're planning to cut all the way through it — you certainly don't want to end up cutting into your work table or workbench.

Adjust the position. Here's where you can really appreciate the adjustment ability of the jig. Once you've mounted your router to the base plate and have inserted your bit (typically a straight bit), you can slide the router back and forth along the rod to the exact position by simply moving the wing nuts that secure the pivot block to the threaded rod. Once you've fine-tuned the location, give the wing nuts a final twist to lock them in place against the pivot block.

Rout the circle. Now for the fun: Set your router bit for a light pass (usually ¼" deep), turn it on, and plunge the bit into the workpiece. Gently guide the router in a clockwise direction to make the cut until you've gone full circle. Use a sharp bit and do not force the cut: This could cause the rod to flex, producing a less-than-perfect circle. Repeat this procedure, increasing the depth of cut until you've cut all the way through the workpiece.

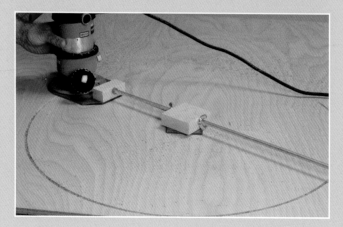

SMALL CIRCLE JIG

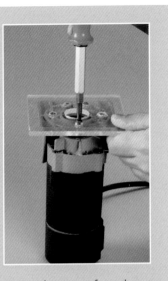

The circle jig featured on pages 136–138 is great for cutting large circles. But it's limited in how small a circle it can cut. If you need to cut, say, a 3" or 4" circle, you can make a simple circle-cutting base plate for your router. This is just a clear acrylic base plate mounted to the router with a pivot pin installed directly on it.

Attach acrylic base to router. Start by cutting the desired size acrylic base plate for your router. Cut it oversized to allow for some adjustment of the pivot pin. Use the original base plate to mark the mounting holes and bit opening. Drill these and countersink the mounting holes. Then attach the acrylic base to the router with the original mounting screws (see the photo at right).

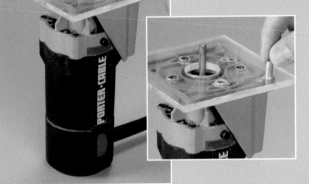

Add the pivot pin. Next, insert a bit into the router and measure from the inside of the bit to the desired radius as shown, and mark the pin location on the base plate; see the photo at left. (Measure from the outside of the bit if you're cutting a hole and not a circle.) Then drill a ¼" hole in the base plate for a piece of ¼" metal rod. You can use a smaller-diameter pin if desired, but the smaller they are, the more they tend to flex and cause the base to jump off the pin and ruin the cut. Now insert the pin into the hole you drilled in the base plate (inset). Secure it with 5-minute epoxy, taking care to remove any squeeze-out immediately.

Rout the circle. When the epoxy has cured, drill a ¼" hole centered in your workpiece. (Remember to slip a scrap piece under your workpiece if you're routing all the way through; it's also a good idea to fasten the circle you're cutting to this scrap to prevent it from moving around and ruining the edge once it's cut free.) Then set your router for a light pass (¼" deep), and position the router so the pivot pin is aligned with the hole in the workpiece. Turn on the router and slip the pin into the hole; rout in a clockwise direction for a full 360 degrees (bottom photo). Repeat as necessary until the final depth is achieved.

Router Bit Cabinet

Router bits are expensive — especially carbide-tipped bits. A $^1/_2$"-shank carbide-tipped quality bit can run anywhere from $30 to $75. With the average wood-worker owning at least a dozen bits or so, this adds up to serious money — often much more than the cost of the router — and it's certainly an investment worth protecting. Many users keep their bits in the original packaging, but this gets bulky and can make it a real chore to find the right bit. Others simply let them rattle around in a drawer or plastic container, which will lead to chipped carbide and dull edges.

A good solution is the router bit cabinet shown here. It provides instant access to your bits while fully pro-tecting them. Sliding Plexiglas doors keep the bits clean while offering a clear view of your bits. A set of angled bit holders tilt the bits out slightly to make them easy to remove and insert.

But what you can't see about the bit holders is what's really handy — all the holes are $^5/_8$" diameter to accept round plastic spacers. These spacers are avail-able in $^1/_4$" and $^1/_2$" inner diameters, so you can mix and match to fit your bits. You don't have to custom-drill holes to

EXPLODED VIEW

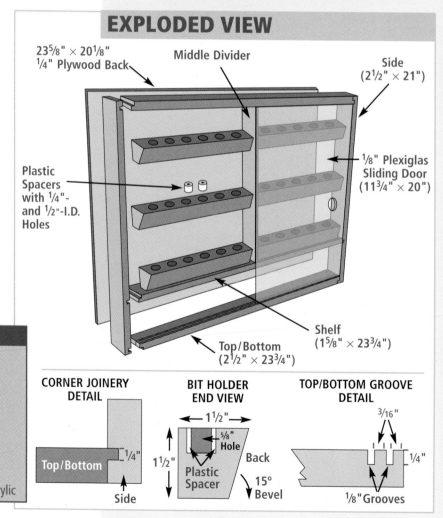

23$^5/_8$" × 20$^1/_8$"
$^1/_4$" Plywood Back

Middle Divider

Side
(2$^1/_2$" × 21")

Plastic
Spacers
with $^1/_4$"-
and $^1/_2$"-I.D.
Holes

$^1/_8$" Plexiglas
Sliding Door
(11$^3/_4$" × 20")

Shelf
(1$^5/_8$" × 23$^3/_4$")

Top/Bottom
(2$^1/_2$" × 23$^3/_4$")

CORNER JOINERY DETAIL

Top/Bottom

Side

$^1/_4$"

BIT HOLDER END VIEW

1$^1/_2$"

$^5/_8$"
Hole

Back

Plastic
Spacer

1$^1/_2$"

15°
Bevel

TOP/BOTTOM GROOVE DETAIL

$^3/_{16}$"

$^1/_4$"

$^1/_8$" Grooves

MATERIALS LIST

Part	Quantity	Dimensions
Sides	2	2$^1/_2$" × 21" − $^3/_4$"
Top/bottom	2	2$^1/_2$" × 23$^3/_4$" − $^3/_4$"
Back	1	23$^5/_8$" × 20$^1/_8$" − $^1/_4$"
Shelves	2	1$^5/_8$" × 23$^3/_4$" − $^3/_4$"
Bit holders	6	1$^1/_2$" × 11$^1/_4$" − 1$^1/_2$"
Divider	1	1$^5/_8$" × 15$^1/_4$" − $^3/_4$"
Doors	2	11$^3/_4$" × 20" − $^1/_8$" acrylic

fit the bits; just swap out the spacers. And because they're plastic, they won't shrink or swell, so bits will always slip in and out with ease. A long shelf beneath the bit holders provides storage for bits that won't fit in the holders (such as large panel-raising bits), plus extra collets and a wrench or two.

Rout the grooves in the sides

The cabinet case is joined with a locking rabbet joint. Grooves are cut in the sides to accept the tongues that are formed by rabbeting the top and bottom pieces, see the corner joinery detail in the drawing on the opposite page. Rout these $1/4$"-wide, $1/4$"-deep grooves $1/2$" in from each end of both side pieces (top photo). Then cut a similar groove 5" up from the bottom end of each side to accept the shelf that'll be added later.

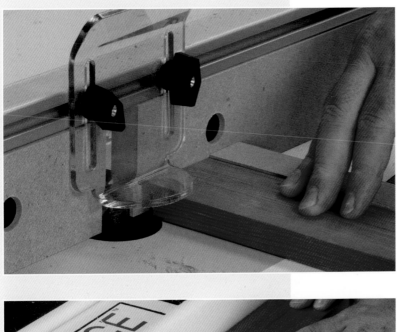

Rout rabbets in top, bottom, and shelf

Next, cut or rout the rabbets on the ends of the top, bottom, and shelf pieces to fit into the grooves you just cut in the sides (middle photo). Make a test cut or two on a scrap piece until the tongue just slips into the groove. A $3/8$" or $1/2$" straight bit works best for this when fitted in the router table; set the fence to produce a $1/4$"-long tongue and use a miter gauge to guide the cut. Make sure to use a backer block to prevent chip-out (see page 98 for more on this).

Cut door grooves

With corner joinery complete, you can cut the grooves along the front edges of the top and bottom pieces to accept the sliding doors (see the groove detail on the opposite page). These $1/8$"-wide, $1/4$"-deep grooves are easily cut on the table saw (bottom photo). They're $3/16$" in from the edge and are $3/16$" apart.

Rout rabbet for back

The $1/4$" plywood back fits into rabbets routed into the back inside edges of the sides and top and bottom. Cut or rout the $1/4$"-deep, $3/8$"-wide rabbet on the table saw fitted with a dado blade or with a router and rabbeting or straight bit. If you're routing the rabbet, consider making a light first pass or backrouting to prevent tear-out (see pages 100–101 for more on this).

Assemble the case

Now you can assemble the case. Start by brushing glue into the grooves in the sides and onto the tongues on the top, bottom, and shelf. Clamp the cabinet together, making sure it's square by measuring the diagonals and comparing (middle photo). Allow the glue to dry and then add the back. Secure the back with glue and brads. Finally, cut and install the divider that fits between the top and the shelf. This can be secured with glue and screws driven in through the back and into the shelf.

Make the bit holders

The bit holders are best cut to size on the table saw. Tilt the blade to 15 degrees and bevel-rip each holder, taking care to use a push block and a featherboard to press the blank firmly against the rip fence (bottom photo). To determine the exact length of the holders, measure between the center divider and each side and then cut the holders to length. In our cabinet, they are $11^{1}/4$" long.

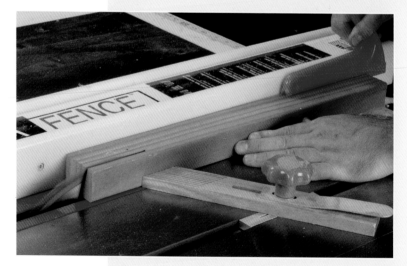

Drill the holes for the spacers

Next, lay out eight evenly spaced holes on each holder for the plastic spacers. These are $5/8$"-diameter holes, and they're located $1/2$" in from the front (non-beveled) edge; see the Bit Holder End View on page 140. The best tool for drilling these holes is the drill press, as you're guaranteed that the holes will be perfectly vertical. Alternatively, drill them with a portable drill as shown, clamping each securely to the work surface. These holes will then accept the plastic spacers (right photo).

Attach bit holders to back

The bit holders are secured to the back with glue and screws driven in through the back and into each holder. Place one set of holders so they rest on top of the shelf. Then position the remaining holders so they're evenly spaced above the bottom holder.

Make and attach the doors

All that's left to complete the cabinet is to cut two sliding doors to fit and then drill finger holes in each door. These 1"-diameter holes are located $1^1/2$" in from the side edges and 9" up from the bottom. A hole saw will work best for drilling these. Insert the top edge of a door into one of the grooves cut in the top of the cabinet and then, if necessary, flex it slightly so the lower edge pops into the groove in the bottom. Repeat for the remaining door. Slip the plastic spacers into the bit holders and add your router bits.

Box-Joint Jig

Although many woodworkers cut box joints on the table saw fitted with a dado blade, there's a better tool for the job: the router. That's because a straight bit in a router will cut a perfectly flat-bottomed notch — something you just can't do with any saw or dado blade. The tooth configurations of the blades will always produce some unevenness, but this isn't so with a straight bit.

In order to cut box joints, you'll need a jig to accurately space the notches apart. The box-joint jig shown here attaches to your miter gauge and features an adjustable front plate that slides back and forth on the slotted back. This makes adjusting the spacing a simple task. The two halves of the jig are joined with a spline that runs along the length of each piece. A threaded stud locks the two parts together once the spacing has been perfected. There are a number of materials you can use for the index pin that the workpiece slips over during use (see page 147), but we chose a short length of square metal bar since it holds up the best.

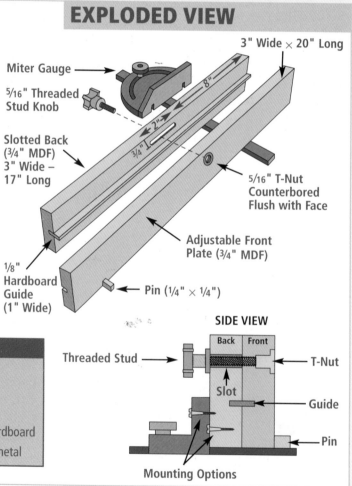

EXPLODED VIEW

3" Wide × 20" Long

Miter Gauge

5/16" Threaded Stud Knob

Slotted Back (3/4" MDF) 3" Wide – 17" Long

8"

2"

3/4"

5/16" T-Nut Counterbored Flush with Face

Adjustable Front Plate (3/4" MDF)

1/8" Hardboard Guide (1" Wide)

Pin (1/4" × 1/4")

SIDE VIEW

Back   Front

Threaded Stud

T-Nut

Slot

Guide

Pin

Mounting Options

MATERIALS LIST

Part	Quantity	Dimensions
Slotted back	1	3" × 17" – 3/4"
Front plate	1	3" × 20" – 3/4"
Guide strip	1	1" × 17" – 1/8" hardboard
Pin	1	1/4" × 1 1/2" – 1/4" metal

Cut guide strip groove

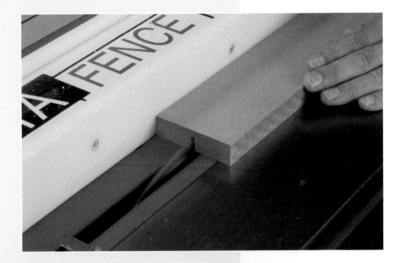

To build the box-joint jig, start by cutting matching grooves in the adjustable front plate and slotted back for the guide. Since the guide is a strip of $1/8$" hardboard, the $1/8$"-wide groove is best cut on the table saw as shown at left. The groove is slightly deeper than $1/2$" to provide a bit of clearance so the guide won't bind in the grooves.

Rout slot in back

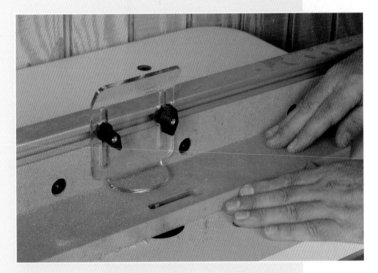

The simplest way to rout the slot in the back that lets you slide the front plate back and forth is to start by laying out and drilling a pair of $5/16$" holes to define the ends (see the drawing on the opposite page). This way, you can fit your table-mounted router with a $1/4$" straight bit and lower the back onto the bit without needing to make a plunge cut. Position the fence $3/4$" away from the center of the bit. Take three $1/4$" passes to cut through the back, moving the workpiece from right to left each pass. Then adjust the fence to create a $5/16$"-wide slot and take three passes to widen the slot.

Locate the T-nut

The back and front are held together via a threaded stud knob that passes through the back and threads into a T-nut installed in the front plate. To locate this T-nut, temporarily slip the guide strip in place. With the ends of the front and back flush at one end, insert a $5/16$"-diameter brad-point bit in the slot in the back as shown. Tap the brad-point bit with a hammer: The point of the bit will leave a dimple exactly where the center of the T-nut needs to be.

Drill the holes for the T-nut

There are two holes that need to be drilled for the T-nut. First, drill a 3/8" hole through the front plate to accept the body of the T-nut (top photo). Then, drill a 1/8"-deep counterbore on the front face of the plate so that when the T-nut is installed, it won't protrude and interfere with the workpiece. Drill the 5/16" hole with a brad-point bit and the larger counterbore (most likely 1") with a Forstner bit.

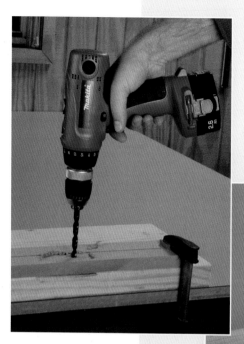

Install the T-nut

Now you can install the T-nut in the front face of the adjustable front plate. Center it in the 3/8" hole and pound it in with a hammer until it sits below the surface of the front plate. Alternatively, you could use a threaded insert here, but the T-nut will provide the best grip without worry about pulling out if it's tightened too much — which threaded inserts are prone to do.

Glue guide strip in the back

To complete the box-joint jig, cut the guide strip to length to match the length of the slotted back and glue it into the back. Make sure to immediately clean up any glue squeeze-out, which would interfere with the sliding motion of the two parts.

Attach the jig to your miter gauge

Before you can use the box-joint jig, there are a couple of preliminary setup steps to do. Start by attaching the jig to your miter gauge. To do this, first slip the miter gauge in the track in the router table top. Position the jig on the miter gauge so that the adjustable front plate extends about 2" past a straight bit installed in the router table. Most miter gauges have a pair of holes in the back for securing auxiliary fences or jigs such as this.

Rout the notch for the index pin

Now you can rout the notch to accept the index pin. The pin should match the size of the box joints you're planning to make, typically, $1/4$", $3/8$", or $1/2$". Set the bit height to match the thickness of the material you'll be joining. For example, set it $1/4$" high (as shown in the photo at left) to join $1/4$"-thick material. Then turn on the router and slide the jig past the bit. It will cut a perfect notch to accept your index pin.

Attach the index pin

Turn off the router and flip the box-joint jig upside down. Cut an index pin to length and epoxy it into the notch you just cut, making sure to immediately wipe off any epoxy squeeze-out. Allow the epoxy to fully set, and you're ready to cut box joints.

INDEX PIN MATERIALS

There are a number of suitable materials to use as an index pin for your box-joint jig. In order of toughness and durability, they are (from left to right in the photo): wood, UHMV plastic, and metal. If you decide to use a metal pin as we did, you need to know that metal bar stock is usually available only in $1/8$" increments. You can find pre-cut lengths in the hardware aisle in most hardware stores; they're often sold as square keys.

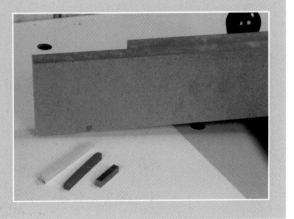

USING THE BOX-JOINT JIG

When it's time to cut box joints, you'll find it easiest if the width of your workpiece is an even increment of the width of the notches you're cutting. This way you'll end up with a full notch or pin at the end of the workpiece.

Cut the first notch. The quickest way to adjust the spacing of the box-joint jig is to use the drill bit tip shown on page 114. Then use a scrap piece to make the first set of cuts. Position the workpiece vertically on the jig so the edge butts up against the index pin as shown. Then turn on the router and push the jig and workpiece past the spinning bit to cut the first notch. Make sure to keep the workpiece constantly pressed up against the index pin.

Shift over for the next cut. Now, simply lift the workpiece and slip the notch you just cut over the index pin. Push the workpiece and jig past the spinning bit to cut the second notch. Repeat as necessary, lifting and dropping on the index pin until all the notches are cut in the workpiece.

Rout the mating part. The notches cut in the mating part must be offset the width of the index pin so the notches will fit over the pins cut in the first piece. The most reliable way to offset the mating piece is to use the mating part as shown in the photo. Slip the first piece over the index pin and butt the mating piece up against it. Turn on the router and rout the first notch. Then butt the notch you just cut in the mating piece against the index pin and continue routing the remaining notches as you did for the first piece.

Router Table

Turn your portable router into a shaper? That's exactly the idea behind a router table. By flipping the router upside down and mounting it to a stand-alone table, you open up a world of new woodworking techniques. You'll be able to do things that just aren't possible with a portable router, such as making vertical raised panels, cope-and-stick joinery, and box joints, to name a few.

The only problem with mounting the router directly to the tabletop? It makes changing and adjusting bits a hassle, since you'd have to get on your knees to

access the collet. That's why the router table shown here uses a drop-in plate. An opening is cut in the tabletop to accept the plate that attaches to the router. This way, all you have to do to change or adjust a bit is to lift the router up and out.

A router table should be sturdy to handle steady use and heavy to dampen vibration. That's why we used a double layer of ³/₄"-thick MDF (medium-density fiberboard) for the top and then covered it top and bottom with plastic laminate. The base of the cabinet is made of 1³/₄"-thick oak and is joined with hardy but easy-to-cut half-laps. The fence shown on page 156 is designed to fit this table.

EXPLODED VIEW

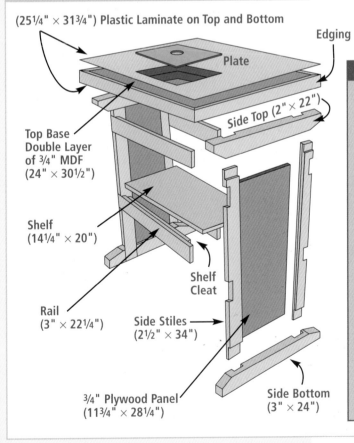

(25¹/₄" × 31³/₄") Plastic Laminate on Top and Bottom

Edging

Plate

Side Top (2" × 22")

Top Base Double Layer of ³/₄" MDF (24" × 30¹/₂")

Shelf (14¹/₄" × 20")

Shelf Cleat

Rail (3" × 22¹/₄")

Side Stiles (2¹/₂" × 34")

³/₄" Plywood Panel (11³/₄" × 28¹/₄")

Side Bottom (3" × 24")

MATERIALS LIST

Part	Quantity	Dimensions
BASE		
Side stiles	4	2¹/₂" × 34" − 1"
Side tops	2	2" × 22" − 1³/₄"
Side bottoms	2	3" × 24" − 1³/₄"
Side panels	2	11³/₄" × 28¹/₄" − ³/₄"
Rails	4	3" × 22¹/₄" − ³/₄"
Shelf	1	14¹/₄" × 20" − ³/₄"
Shelf cleats	2	1" × 20" − ³/₄"
TOP		
Top base	2	24" × 30¹/₂" − ³/₄"
Side edging	2	1¹/₂" × 25¹/₄" − ⁵/₈"
Fr./bk. edging	2	1¹/₂" × 31³/₄" − ⁵/₈"
Laminate	2	25¹/₄" × 31³/₄" *
Plate	1	8¹/₄" × 12" − ³/₈" acrylic
		* (acrylic: cut oversized)

Cut side top and bottom half-laps

Start construction on the router table by cutting one-half of the half-lap joint that joins the side top and bottom to the side stiles. These notches are cut to match the width of the side stiles (2½" wide) and are ½" deep. The quickest way to cut these is with a table saw fitted with a dado blade as shown. Alternatively, you can rout these with your portable router (see pages 67 for more on this).

Cut matching half-laps in stiles

Next, cut the matching half-laps in the ends of the side stiles. The tongue formed on the tops of the side stiles is 2" long and the tongue at the bottom of the side stiles is 3" long to match the respective widths of the side top and bottom. Here again, a table saw fitted with a dado blade will make quick work of this.

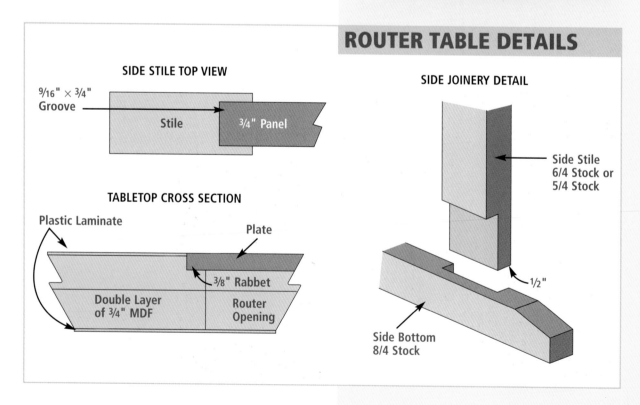

ROUTER TABLE DETAILS

SIDE STILE TOP VIEW

$9/16" \times 3/4"$ Groove

Stile

¾" Panel

TABLETOP CROSS SECTION

Plastic Laminate

Plate

⅜" Rabbet

Double Layer of ¾" MDF

Router Opening

SIDE JOINERY DETAIL

Side Stile 6/4 Stock or 5/4 Stock

½"

Side Bottom 8/4 Stock

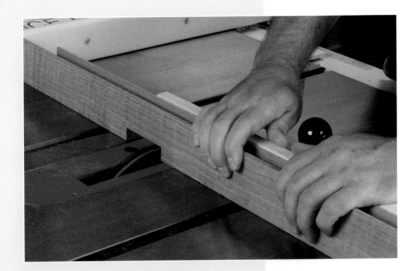

Make notches for the rails

The two side assemblies are connected by a set of horizontal rails that fit into notches cut in the side stiles (see the Exploded View on page 149). These notches are cut to match the thickness and width. These can easily be cut on the table saw using the rip fence as a stop to define the limits of each notch. Then it's just a matter of cleaning out the waste between the two end cuts.

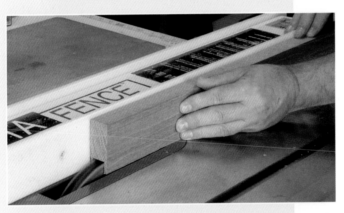

Cut panel grooves in rails

For added strength and to prevent the side assemblies from racking under heavy use, $3/4$"-thick plywood panels fit into grooves cut on the inside edges of the stiles. These grooves are $9/16$" deep and run the full length of each side stile. You can cut these in a single pass using a dado blade fitted in the table saw, or with multiple passes using a router fitted with a straight bit.

Taper ends of side top and bottoms

For appearance, cut a taper on the ends of the side top and bottom pieces. Measure 1" down and 3" over for the taper on each piece. Then cut the taper on the band saw or with a saber saw, and sand the edges smooth. You'll also find it easiest at this time to pre-drill a set of mounting holes about 1" in from the ends of the side tops for mounting the tabletop later.

Assemble the sides

Now you can begin assembling the sides. Start by temporarily clamping the top and bottom pieces to the stiles to form a side. Measure the height and width for the panel that fits in the grooves, and cut a side panel to size. Repeat for the other side. Apply glue to the grooves in the sides, slip in the panel, and apply glue to both sides of the half-laps, joining the top and bottom to the stiles. Check for square and adjust as necessary. Apply clamps to the joints and let dry overnight. Repeat for the remaining side.

Connect sides with rails

With the side assemblies complete, you can join them together with the rails (middle photo). Work on one side at a time and apply glue to the notches cut in the side stiles. Then insert a rail and make sure it's flush with the face of the side stiles. Drill pilot holes and fasten the rails to the side assemblies with #8 × 2 1/2" flathead woodscrews. Tip: For a finished appearance, use finishing or countersinking washers, sold at most home centers in the hardware aisle.

Add edging to the top base

Now that the base is done, you can turn your attention to the top. The top consists of a double layer of 3/4"-thick MDF (medium-density fiberboard) wrapped with 5/8"-thick edging and covered top and bottom with plastic laminate. Begin by cutting the MDF to size. Then glue the two layers together with contact cement, making sure the edges are flush around the entire perimeter. Then miter-cut the edging to wrap around the top base and secure it with glue and clamps. For added strength, consider fastening the edging with biscuits.

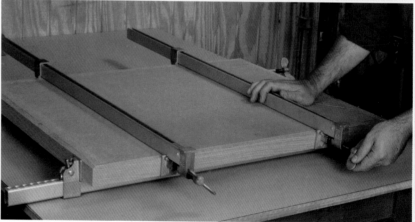

Attach laminate to the top

After the glue on the edging has dried, the next step is to apply plastic laminate to both sides of the top. This may seem like a waste of laminate, but covering the bottom helps prevent the MDF on the bottom from taking on moisture and warping the top. Cut the laminate at least 1" oversized in both directions. Apply a generous coat of contact cement to both the MDF and the laminate; allow it to gloss over (top photo). Then lay scraps of wood or dowels on the MDF and carefully position the laminate over the MDF. Remove the center dowel and work from the center out, pressing the laminate in place and continuing to remove dowels until the laminate is in place. Then press it down firmly with a laminate roller or rolling pin.

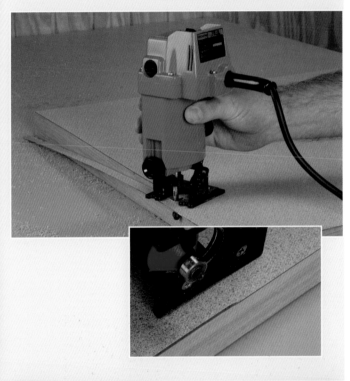

Rout the laminate

As soon as the laminate is pressed in place, you can trim it to fit. That's the beauty of contact cement. Fit your router or laminate trimmer with a flush-trim bit, and run this around the perimeter of the top to trim the laminate to match the top (middle photo). Do this for both sides. Then, insert a chamfer bit in the router and rout a slight chamfer around the top and bottom perimeter (inset). This not only looks good, but it also helps prevent a workpiece from catching on the edges as it's fed past the router.

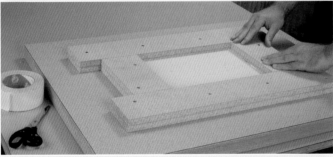

Lay out location of router plate

Cutting the opening in the router table can be tricky, so take your time here. The most accurate way to create this opening is to use the router plate itself to define the opening and cut the opening with a patternmaker's bit (for more on this, see page 29). Here's how to do it. Start by making a set of guides. These are just scraps of MDF or particleboard cut to wrap around the plate (bottom photo). The depth of the groove you'll cut with the patternmaker's bit around the perimeter needs to match the thickness of your router plate. With this in mind, you'll likely need to make the guides at least 1" thick. Position the plate where you want it on the tabletop and position the guides around it as shown. Secure the guides to the table with strips of double-sided carpet tape.

Rout opening for plate

Now remove the router plate and set the depth of your patternmaker's bit to make a cut to match the thickness of the router plate. It's a good idea to test this setup first on a piece of scrap. Then turn on your router and gently lower it into the top; make sure you press the bearing firmly against the guide strips. Rout all the way around the perimeter to form a groove.

Cut out the opening

Now what you've really cut in the tabletop is the lip that the router plate will rest on. Your next step is to remove the waste to the *inside* of this lip — in other words, cut an opening for the router. The best way to do this is to start by drilling a set of access holes for a saber saw in each corner. These should be drilled in the waste area as shown — not in the groove you just routed. When you've drilled all four corners, cut away the waste with a saber saw. Leave as much of the lip (groove) as possible as you cut.

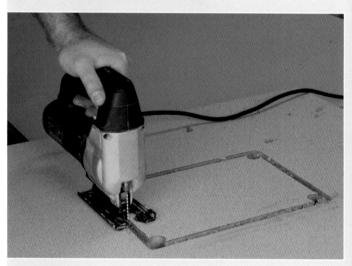

Make the router plate

With the waste removed, check to make sure the router plate fits snugly in the groove; adjust as necessary. Note: Since the patternmaker's bit leaves a rounded corner, you can either round over the corners of the router plate (the easier choice) or square up the corners of the opening. Either way, use your router's original base plate to mark mounting holes and bit opening in the router plate, and drill these holes.

Attach the router

Attach your router to the router plate with the original mounting screws. Then secure the tabletop to the base with $1/4$" lag screws driven up though the holes you drilled previously in the side tops and into the top. It's best to mark and drill holes in the underside of the top before driving in the lag screws. Then set the router and router plate into the opening in the tabletop (inset). Note: On some larger plunge routers, you may find that you'll first need to remove the handles in order for it to fit in the opening you cut in the top. This won't affect the router's ability to perform properly in the router table, since the handles won't be used.

TABLE SAW ROUTER

If space is at a premium in your shop, consider making just the table portion of this router table and mounting it in place of one of the wing extensions of your table saw (see the drawing below). An added benefit of this setup is that you don't have to build a separate fence — you can use the rip fence of your table saw. You will have to alter the dimensions of the top to fit your saw, but cutting the opening for the plate remains the same.

Alternatively, a number of enterprising router accessory manufacturers offer pre-made tables designed to fit a variety of saws (see the photo below right). The table insert shown bottom right is manufactured by Bench Dog and is available at www.benchdog.com.

MOUNTING A ROUTER TABLE

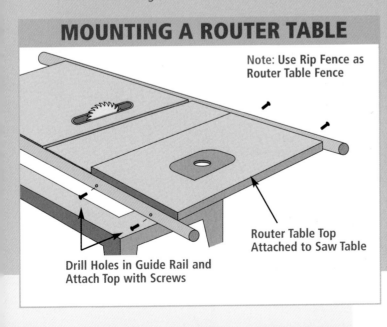

Note: Use Rip Fence as Router Table Fence

Router Table Top Attached to Saw Table

Drill Holes in Guide Rail and Attach Top with Screws

Router Table Fence

The very first router table fence was most likely a strip of wood clamped to the table. This worked, but adjusting the strip, particularly fine-tuning it, was a real pain. There's also no provision for cuts that require the bit to be buried in the fence, such as when cutting a rabbet with a straight bit. Granted, you could cut a notch in the strip of wood, but then it would work only for that individual bit.

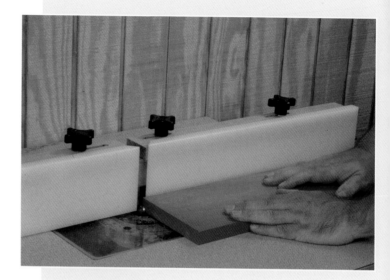

That's why a truly useful fence for the router table should be easy to position, have an adjustable bit opening, and be solid and reliable. Combine these features and you have the fence shown here. Built-in clamps on the sides make positioning the fence a snap. The bit opening is fully adjustable — just slide a set of fence faces back and forth. Accuracy is provided by a unique metal rod guide system that ensures that the faces will always track in line with each other. For the ultimate in fence faces, we chose $3/4$"-thick UHMW plastic. The plastic faces are absolutely flat, and a workpiece will slide along them as if they were lubricated.

EXPLODED VIEW

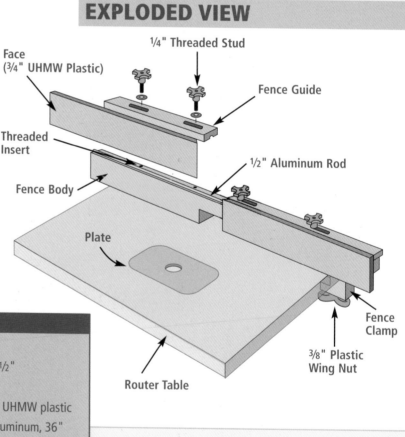

Face (3/4" UHMW Plastic)

1/4" Threaded Stud

Fence Guide

Threaded Insert

Fence Body

1/2" Aluminum Rod

Plate

Fence Clamp

3/8" Plastic Wing Nut

Router Table

MATERIALS LIST

Part	Quantity	Dimensions
Fence body	1	$2^3/4$" × 36" – $1^1/2$"
Fence guides	2	2" × 18" – $3/4$"
Fence faces	2	4" × 18" – $3/4$" UHMW plastic
Rod	1	$1/2$"-diameter aluminum, 36"
Fence clamp	2	$2^3/8$" × $2^7/8$" – $1^3/4$"
Fence spline	2	$1^1/4$" × $1^3/4$" – $1/4$" hardboard
Plate	1	8" × 11" – $1/4$" acrylic

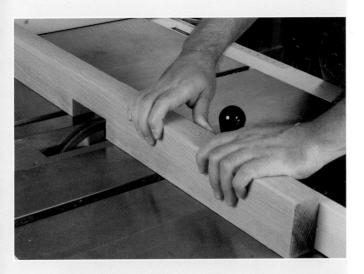

Cut the bit opening in the body

We chose 1³/₄"-thick oak for the fence body as it's dense, heavy, and flat. The first thing to do with the body is to cut an oversized opening for the bit. This then will be covered by the adjustable faces. A table saw fitted with a dado blade works best for this cut because you can set the rip fence as a stop and guide the piece with the miter gauge. The notch is 1¹/₂" high and 3" wide.

Rout grooves for rod

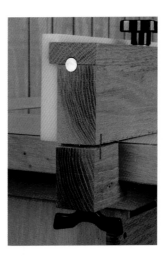

The fence guides and faces slide back and forth against the body. These are kept in alignment via a ¹/₂" aluminum rod that fits in a set of matching grooves cut in the top of the body and the underside of the fence guides (inset). A ¹/₂" core-box bit set for a ¹/₂"-deep cut works best for this (you may want to take two ¹/₄"-deep cuts instead). Set up a temporary fence by clamping a straight strip of wood to your router table 1¹/₄" away from the center of the bit. Rout matching grooves in the body and guides, taking care to press the back edge of each piece against the temporary fence.

Rout slots in the guides

The fence guides are locked in place by a set of threaded studs that pass through the guides and into threaded inserts in the fence body. You'll need to rout two slots in each guide for these studs. The easiest way to rout these is to first drill ¹/₄" holes to define the ends of the slots and then remove the waste between them with the router, as shown. These slots are ¹/₂" in from the back edge, 2" long, and located 1" and 6", respectively, from the ends of the guides.

Locate insert holes

To locate the threaded inserts in the fence body, temporarily place the aluminum rod in the groove in the body and set the fence guides in place so the ends are flush with the body. Then insert a $1/4$" brad-point bit in the end of the slot as shown and tap it with a hammer. This will create a dimple at the exact center of the insert.

Install the inserts

Remove the fence guides and aluminum rod and drill the recommended-sized holes for the inserts. Depending on the type of insert you're using, they'll need to be either screwed in or hammered in placed like those shown here. Make sure to guide the insert carefully so it goes in vertical. Also, the insert must end up slightly below the surface of the fence body to ensure that it won't catch on the fence guides.

FENCE DETAILS

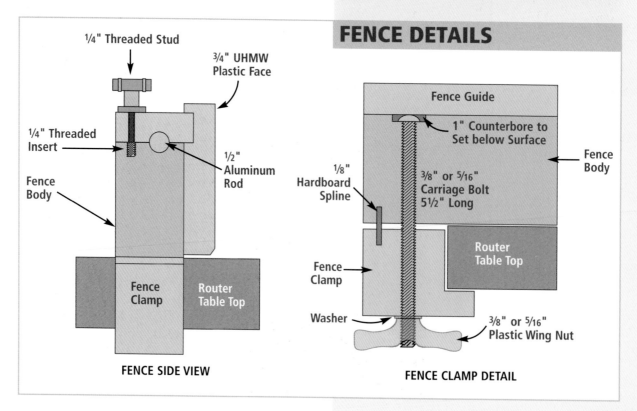

FENCE SIDE VIEW

- $1/4$" Threaded Stud
- $3/4$" UHMW Plastic Face
- $1/4$" Threaded Insert
- $1/2$" Aluminum Rod
- Fence Body
- Fence Clamp
- Router Table Top

FENCE CLAMP DETAIL

- Fence Guide
- 1" Counterbore to Set below Surface
- Fence Body
- $1/8$" Hardboard Spline
- $3/8$" or $5/16$" Carriage Bolt $5 1/2$" Long
- Router Table Top
- Fence Clamp
- Washer
- $3/8$" or $5/16$" Plastic Wing Nut

Cut grooves in fence faces

Now that the guides are complete, you can make the fence faces. Although we used UHMW plastic here, you could certainly use $3/4$"-thick MDF or plywood for the faces instead. Cut these to size and then cut a groove on the inside face $1/4$" down from the top edge on each face. These grooves are $1/4$" deep and sized to match the thickness of the fence guide ($3/4$"). You can cut these on the table saw fitted with a dado blade, or with a router fitted with a straight bit.

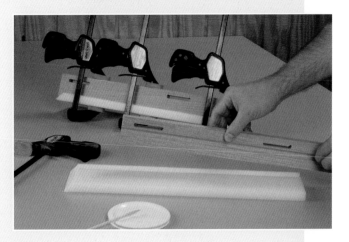

Glue the faces to the guides

There are two more steps before you can glue the faces to the fence guides. First, miter-cut the inside ends of the fence faces that will cover the bit opening. This allows the faces to come closer in on some types of bits. Second, rout a $3/16$" chamfer along the bottom edge of each fence face to serve as sawdust relief. Glue the faces to the fence guides, making sure the ends are flush. With UHMW plastic, you'll need to use epoxy for this. Make sure you end up with a right-handed and left-handed fence.

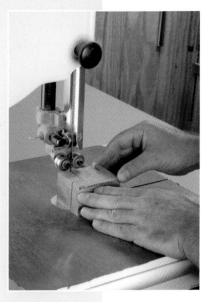

Cut the fence clamps to size

All that's left is to make the fence clamps that secure the fence to the router table top (see the construction detail drawings on the opposite page). Cut the fence clamps from $1^{1}/2$" stock and then cut the notch in each end to fit over your table. Note: The dimensions shown here are for clamps that fit the table featured on pages 149–155. You'll need to alter the notch size if you use a different top. Cut the notch out with a hand saw, saber saw, or band saw.

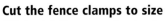

Cut matching grooves for splines

The fence clamps are tightened in place by a carriage bolt that passes through the body and plastic wing nut on the bottom. To create a gap that can be closed when the wing nut is tightened and to prevent the fence clamp from twisting when secured, cut matching grooves (kerfs, actually) in the underside of the fence body and top on the fence clamps. These grooves accept splines added later. The kerfs are $1/8$" wide and $1/2$" deep. They're located $1/2$" in from the ends of the fence body and fence clamp.

Drill holes for clamp bolts

The next step is to drill holes for the carriage bolts to pass through the fence clamps and the fence body. Drill the hole in the fence clamp first and then clamp this to the underside of the fence body. Use the fence clamp as a guide to start the hole in the fence body; this will guarantee alignment. Remove the fence clamp and drill completely through the fence body. Repeat for the opposite end. Finally, drill a 1" counterbore in the top of the fence body with a Forstner bit to allow the head of the carriage bolt to sit below the surface. This way, it won't interfere with the sliding fence guide.

Attach clamps to body

the holes have been drilled, insert a carriage bolt in each end. Slip a $1\,1/4$"-wide spline in each groove cut in the fence body, and then slide a fence clamp over the bolt. Add a washer and a plastic wing nut and temporarily tighten the wing nut to pull the head of the carriage bolt into the body. Loosen the wing nut, and it's ready to go onto the table.

Attach guides to fence body
Now you can install the aluminum rod in the fence body and position the fence guides on top. Thread the threaded studs through the slot in the fence guides and tighten.

USING THE FENCE

Position the fence. To adjust the position of the fence, loosen the plastic wing nuts and slide the fence into a rough position. Tighten the wing nuts so they're friction-tight, and fine-tune the position of the fence. Many woodworkers prefer to fully tighten one end of a fence and then fine-tune the position by pivoting the opposite end. This method works fine as long as you're not planning on using the miter gauge. If you are, it's best to leave both ends friction-tight for fine-tuning. When in final position, fully tighten both wing nuts. Note: This takes surprisingly little pressure to clamp the fence in place. Experiment to find how much pressure is enough. Overtightening will only cause undue stress on the splines, clamps, fence body, and tabletop.

Adjust the faces. Adjust the faces as needed for the bit and operation. Close them completely for cuts such as grooves and dadoes that are set in from an edge. Open them to allow for housed cuts. Whenever you can, adjust the faces to be as close to the bit as possible without actually touching it. This will provide the maximum fence surface for guiding a cut.

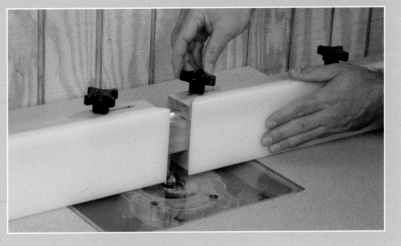

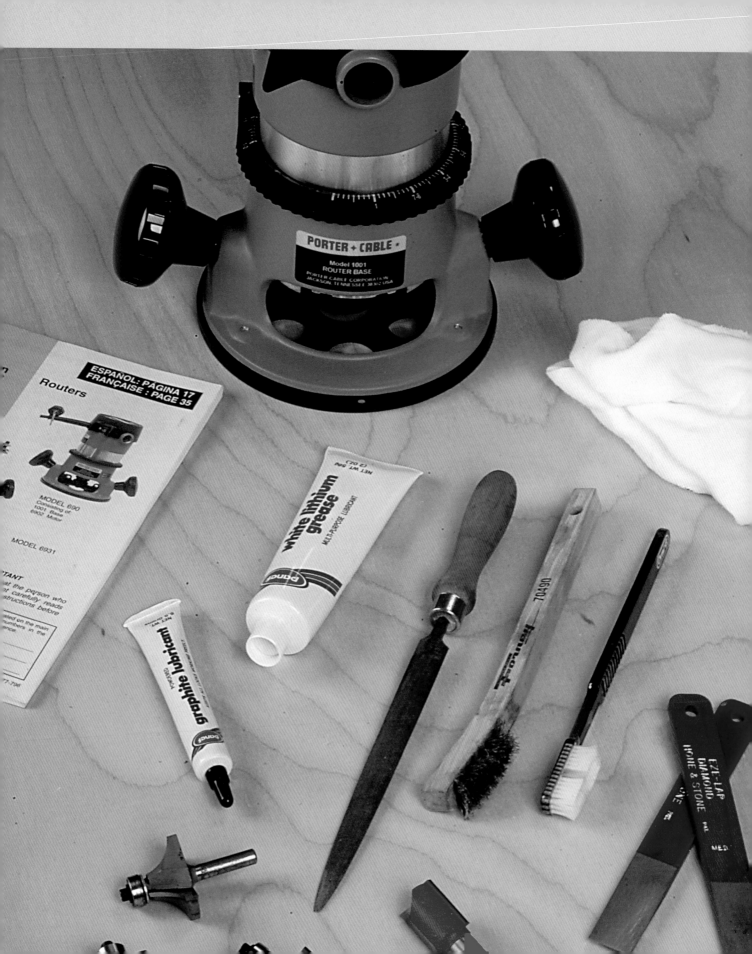

6 Router Maintenance & Troubleshooting

If you gathered together a few dozen woodworkers and asked how many routinely service their routers, you might see one or two hands raised. The rest will look a little embarrassed, and guiltily admit they do little, if any, maintenance. This is a curious thing, since some of them would spend hours tuning and sharpening a hand plane that gets only occasional use, yet they'll completely neglect one of the workhorses in their shop: the router. What's more, a quality router can cost multiples of the hand plane's cost, so protecting this investment seems even more logical.

Part of the blame here is the inherent hardiness of most routers. Like the Energizer bunny, a quality-made router will keep going...and going...so well, in fact, that maintenance is often ignored until a problem occurs. Then you're faced with annoyance, frustration, and cost. The good news is that most problems are preventable. Maintaining a router in tip-top shape requires few tools and materials and takes little time — especially if you follow the guidelines in this chapter and begin a regimen of regular care.

A basic maintenance kit for keeping a router tuned to perfection consists of the owner's manual, a set of brushes and rags for cleaning, white lithium grease and graphite for lubrication, and a couple of different grits and sizes of diamond hones for sharpening.

Inside a Router

Before delving into maintenance, it's important that you familiarize yourself with the various parts of a router. Start by looking in the owner's manual for your router, to find an exploded view diagram and accompanying parts list. Most routers, like the fixed-base router shown in the drawing at right, have two main parts: a motor unit and a base. The motor unit contains the electrical connections (power cord, etc.) and the motor and drive shaft that the collet and/or collet nut attaches to in order to accept a bit. A motor unit commonly consists of a rear and front housing that hold the commutator bearing, field winding, armature, fan, and fan bearing. The rear housing features a pair of brush caps that hold in a pair of spring-loaded brushes that connect power to the rotating armature. The on/off switch may or may not be contained in this unit, although it typically is.

The router base accepts the motor unit and offers some type of height-adjustment mechanism: either a rack-and-pinion, a plunge mechanism complete with rods, or a pin-and-groove system where a pin on the motor unit engages a spiral groove inside the router body. There's also some type of locking mechanism to secure the motor unit in the base once it has been adjusted to the desired depth of cut. On a standard router, this usually involves a split router base that squeezes or clamps the motor unit when the locking knob or lever is activated. With plunge routers, a cam lever pinches one of the guide rods to lock the bit in for the desired cut depth.

The bottom of the base is covered with a plastic or phenolic sub-base that has a cutout for the router bit to pass through. This plastic base

prevents the router from marring the surface of the workpiece. Handles on the side of the router provide the means to guide it during the cut. Most router bases have some type of depth-of-cut indicator, but this should be used only for rough positioning — always make a test cut to sneak up on the final cut.

EXPLODED INTERNAL VIEW OF A ROUTER

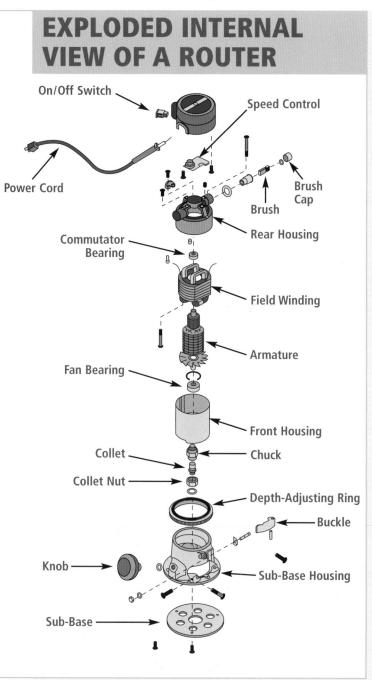

On/Off Switch
Speed Control
Power Cord
Brush Cap
Brush
Rear Housing
Commutator Bearing
Field Winding
Armature
Fan Bearing
Front Housing
Collet
Chuck
Collet Nut
Depth-Adjusting Ring
Buckle
Knob
Sub-Base Housing
Sub-Base

Periodic Cleaning

Like any tool in your shop, the router will benefit from periodic cleaning. The three main areas that need regular attention are the collet, the adjustment mechanism, and the body of the router. Note: Routers mounted upside down in a router table will require the most attention, as they operate under a steady downpour of chips and sawdust.

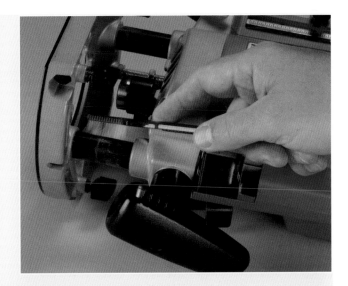

Collet

Of all the parts in a router, the collet works hardest. Without constant cleaning, sawdust and pitch or gum can build up inside the collet and prevent it from gripping the bit securely. You should clean the collet every time you change a bit. All it takes is a blast of air, via a compressor, from a can of compressed air (photo above), or just lung-powered. Keep a can of compressed air near the router bits as a reminder to keep the collet clean.

Adjustment mechanism

Next to the collet, the height-adjustment mechanism on a router gets the most work. The type of adjustment mechanism on your router will determine how you clean it and how often. On a fixed-base router, this could mean keeping the groove in which the pin rotates clean, or keeping the geared rack of a rack-and-pinion mechanism free of dust. With plunge routers, you'll need to remove dust from the plunge rods, and keep dust from accumulating at the top and bottom of the rods (middle photo). An old toothbrush works great for most cleaning jobs like this. Clean the adjustment mechanism before storing it, after use, and anytime you notice built-up sawdust.

Router body

The router body generally needs the least attention. Here again, cleaning it after use is a good idea. Blow off any dust with compressed air or lung power and a soft-bristle brush. Then wipe the body with a clean, soft cloth. Metal parts can be cleaned by dipping a cloth in acetone or lacquer thinner (bottom photo). This will help remove grease and accumulated pitch and gum. Pitch and gum that have built up on plastic parts, such as the knobs or base plate, are best gently scraped off with a sharp utility knife.

Collet Maintenance

If you've ever priced a replacement collet, you know that they're surprisingly expensive. So it's well worth the time and effort to keep these critical parts in perfect condition.

Cleaning

In addition to blowing out a collet regularly (see page 165) to prevent sawdust from building up, it's also a good idea to routinely clean the inside of the collet — the area that really does the work. There are a couple of ways to do this. One is to simply run a soft rag through the collet. If there's any possibility of pitch and gum buildup, dampen the cloth with acetone or lacquer thinner to help remove it. Alternatively, a brass-bristle brush (inset) is a great way to keep the interior of the collet looking like new. You can find these where gun-cleaning supplies are found or at www.woodhaven.com.

Lubrication

The inside of a collet should never be lubricated. Period. Any lubricant at all will prevent the collet from gripping the bit securely. What will benefit from lubrication are the threads of the collet or collet nut that secure the collet to the armature shaft. Before you apply lubricant here, clean the threads thoroughly with an old toothbrush. Then brush on a light coat of grease (middle photo); white lithium grease works well for this, and can be found in most hardware stores and home centers. After brushing on the grease, use a clean, soft cloth to wipe off any excess. What you're after here is a thin, light coat. Any more than this will attract sawdust like a magnet.

Deburring

Just like a drill bit that slips in a drill chuck, a router bit can slip inside a collet in use. Slipping like this will usually cause a burr to form either on the

bit shank or inside the collet. If you have trouble inserting bits into the collet, check with a flashlight for a burr. If you find one, use a needle file (bottom photo) to remove it. Take care to remove the burr without scoring the collet. File gently and check often by inserting a router bit until it slides in easily.

Checking for wear and tear

Over time, some collets will just stop functioning well: Either they don't hold a bit securely, or bits are hard to remove and insert. This is usually the result of two things: repeated overtightening of the collet, and storing the router with a bit tightened in the collet. The end result is that the inner diameter of the collet changes. To check for this, try inserting the shank of a drill bit in the collet that matches its size. The $1/2$" collet shown here is in good condition, as it readily accepts the bit with virtually no side-to-side play.

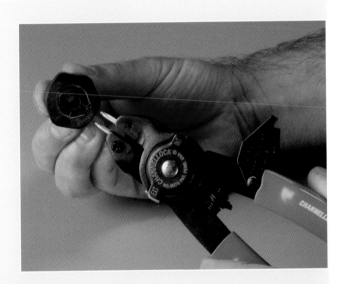

Adjusting collets

A collet that exhibits excessive play will need to be replaced (see below). Some collets can be salvaged — like the split-ring variety common on older Craftsman routers that have "shrunk" over time due to over-tightening. Note: If your collet is a cast or machined unit, this next technique will not work — it will only damage it. To return a split collet to its original inner diameter, try tapping it gently onto an undersized drill bit. That is, for a $1/4$" collet, use a $15/64$" bit. Drill a matching hole in a block of wood and insert the bit with the shank up. Then tap the end of the collet onto the bit to spread it open. If this works, then move up to a $1/4$" bit. Make sure to use a rubber-faced mallet to keep from damaging the edges of the collet.

Replacing a collet

If all else fails, you can replace the collet. In many cases, the collet is secured to a collet nut via a C-clip or snap ring. C-clips can easily be pried off with a screwdriver or awl. Snap rings are best removed with a pair of snap-ring pliers like the pair shown at left. When ordering a replacement collet, it's best to take the collet with you to the tool store. Make sure also to have the model and serial number of the router, as even the same model routers use different collets.

COLLET NUTS AND WRENCHES

Collet nuts. With use, collet nuts often get scarred from a slipped wrench. Remove any burrs with a flat mill file, and sand off any rust with emery cloth. Wipe on a light coat of machine oil and then remove any excess with a clean cloth.

Collet wrenches. Keep collet wrenches in tip-top shape by removing any burrs that form on the jaws of the wrench. Also, take the time to soften the handle edges with a smooth mill file — your hands will appreciate it.

Base Plates

The base plate of a router is an often-overlooked part that does require occasional attention. To slide smoothly over a workpiece, it needs to be clean and smooth.

Check the surface

Even though the plastic on most base plates is high-impact and very tough, it still can get dinged up over time. Typically, this is caused by riding over an exposed screw head or other metal fastener. When this occurs, a burr is usually formed. Often the burr won't be noticeable, but it makes your cuts imperfect. That's because the burr can actually tilt the router slightly, just as if there were a small pebble under it. It makes sense to check the base plate periodically for flatness. Just run the edge of a metal rule gently across the surface (top photo). A burr will cause a catch. When you find one, circle it with a pencil and continue inspecting.

Smoothing a plate

A burr on a base plate can be removed with a couple of different methods. You can slice it off with a hand scraper, file it off with a smooth mill file, or remove it with sandpaper. Since the high-gloss finish of the plastic base plate is easily marred, you'll want to use 600-grit or higher silicon-carbide paper if you elect to sand the burr off, as shown in the middle photo.

Registration

Though not technically maintenance, adding a registration mark to a base plate is a good idea: It serves as a visual guide to keep one point of the base plate in contact with jigs and straightedges when routing. The reason this is necessary is that most router bases aren't perfectly round. So if you rotate the router as you make a guided cut along a straightedge, the cut won't be perfectly parallel to the straightedge (for more on this, see page 175). White nail polish works well for this since it's both durable and highly visible.

Electrical Repairs

There are three typical electrical repairs you can tackle on most routers: replacing a faulty power switch, replacing a frayed electrical cord, and replacing worn-out brushes.

Replacing a power switch

The complexity of replacing a power switch on a router will depend on the manufacturer and the type of switch you're replacing. If it's just a simple on/off switch, it's an easy task. However, if it's a variable-speed switch, it can be more of a challenge since there are usually more wires. There are three basic ways wires are connected to these switches: screws, push-on connectors, and spring clips (see the sidebar below). Start by noting down wire colors and locations before removing the old switch. The most reliable way to replace any power switch is to disconnect one wire at a time and connect it to the corresponding terminal on the replacement switch. Pay particular attention to wire routing, as some wires often run under the switch and can easily be pinched when the case is reassembled.

Replacing a cord

The ease with which you can replace an electrical cord depends primarily on the manufacturer. Some manufacturers have designed the cord so it twists and pulls out for super-easy replacement. Other manufacturers offer detachable housings that provide relatively open access. These are usually held in place with only a couple screws. Regardless of ease of access, once the ends of the cord are in sight, make note of wire colors, locations, and routing. After you've replaced the cord, be careful to route the wires so they don't get pinched when you reassemble the case.

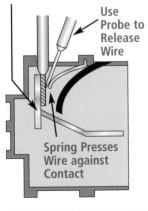

Contact

Use Probe to Release Wire

Spring Presses Wire against Contact

INTERNAL VIEW OF SWITCH

MYSTERY SWITCHES

At first glance, it doesn't appear that the wires going into some switches and other internal electrical parts on a router can be replaced without discombobulating the entire thing. Don't give up: These wires are held in place with a clip inside the switch. All it takes to release the wire is the right tool, such as a dental pick or probe used for assembly/disassembly work (a small nail or thin awl will also get the job done). Probe sets can often be found in the precision-tool section of most hardware stores and tool centers or at electronics parts stores such as Radio Shack. To release the wire, take a straight probe and insert it alongside the wire. This should release the clip, allowing you to pull the wire out. The new wire can usually be re-inserted directly into the hole without using the probe.

Replacing brushes

The brushes in a router motor provide a way to transfer electrical current to a rotating object (in this case, the armature). Brushes are made up of highly conductive carbon particles pressed together in a small rectangular bar. One end of the brush is curved to match the diameter of the armature. A spring inserted between an end cap/wire assembly and brush pushes the brush against the armature. By the very nature of this pressing and rubbing action, the brushes will wear down over time. As the brushes wear and approach the end of their life, you may notice a decrease in power and an accompanying shower of sparks. If even one brush goes completely bad, the motor will stop. Both of these situations call for replacing the brushes. When you do this, keep in mind that you should always replace brushes in pairs.

Good versus bad brushes

If you think you have a brush problem or you'd just like to check them for wear, do a visual inspection. Most routers offer easy access to the brushes by way of a pair of screw-on caps. Remove these with a screwdriver and carefully pull out the brushes. What you're looking for is a nice even gloss on the end of the brush. If it's scarred, it needs to be replaced. As to the length, it's difficult to know when to change brushes unless you know how long they were to start with. As a rule of thumb, if you've got less than 1/4" left in length, replace them.

GOOD VS. BAD BRUSHES

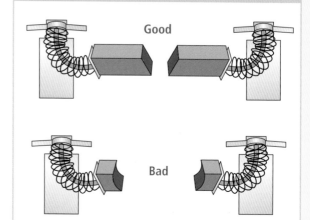

Good

Bad

Compressed springs

Another thing to check brushes for is spring tension. If there isn't enough pressure, the brushes will make intermittent contact and your router will operate sluggishly. If in doubt, replace them. Finally, if you find that your brushes are wearing unevenly or you're replacing them too often, inspect the armature. If one or more of the segments are bad, it can cause excessive brush wear and tear.

COMPRESSED SPRINGS

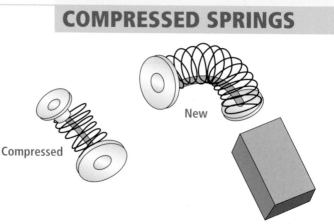

New

Compressed

Height
Adjustment

Regardless of the mechanism, how easy it is to adjust bit height on a router will often depend on how well the adjustment mechanism is maintained. Here's what to do with the three most common types: pin-and-track, rack-and-pinion, and plunge.

Pin-and-track

By its very nature, a pin-and-track adjustment will be subjected to a lot of wear and tear. This is compounded if you remove the motor from the base unit to remove and install bits. Removing the motor doesn't cause problems; it's the remounting that often does. That's because the pin often catches on the insides of the base unit as you try to align the pin with the matching spiral groove. Over time, burrs are bound to form both on the motor housing and inside the base housing. A half-round mill file will quickly remove burrs on both surfaces (top photo).

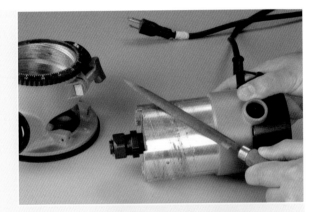

Rack-and-pinion

In any shop, the rack-and-pinion mechanism on a router will slowly acquire a coating of sawdust. This will mix in with any lubricants to form a gooey paste that will eventually make the height difficult to adjust. To prevent this, periodically blow off as much dust as possible with compressed air. If you notice a buildup, scrub away the old goo with a brass-bristle brush or an old toothbrush (middle photo). Then dab a fresh coat of white lithium grease onto the rack with a clean brush and wipe off any excess with a soft rag.

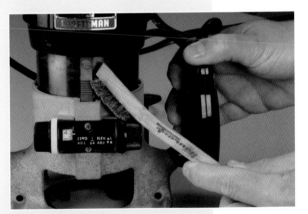

Plunge rods

Lubricating the plunge rods on a plunge router can be sort of a Catch 22. If you lubricate them with oil or grease, they'll attract dust and quickly clog. If you don't use any lubricant, they will stick and bind. The solution is to use a dry lubricant such as graphite. First, clean the rods thoroughly. Then apply a small amount of graphite to a clean rag and rub this on the rods (bottom photo). Spray-on coatings like TopCote work well, too, as long as you spray some on a cloth and apply it to the rods, not directly onto the rods.

Router Table

As with the router, a router table will benefit from routine maintenance and inspection. The three areas to concentrate on are the table surface, the miter gauge and track, and the fence.

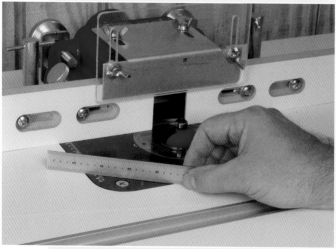

Table surface

For precise routing operations, the router table surface must be clean, flat, and smooth. Periodic cleaning should include brushing or blowing off all dust and wiping down the top with a damp cloth. Any dings or dents should be filled and any high spots removed with a hand scraper or with sandpaper fitted around a sanding block. Before any operation, check to make sure the plate is perfectly level with the top by checking it with a metal rule, as shown in the top photo. Adjust or shim as necessary to prevent the workpiece from catching on the router plate or the lip of the recess the plate fits in.

Miter gauge and track

If your router table has a miter gauge track, check it often for excessive play. Grip the head of the miter gauge as shown in the middle photo, and try to wiggle it from side to side. There should be no play. The only movement should be smooth back and forth as it slides through the track. A loose miter gauge can be corrected by dimpling the sides of the bar with a centerpunch or applying metal tape to one or both sides of the bar. Metal tape, used to seal duct joints, is found in the HVAC aisle at most home centers.

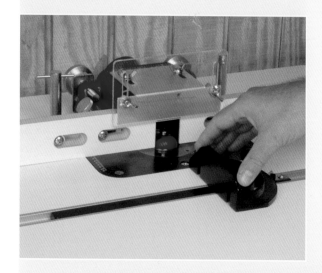

Fence

It's critical for precise cuts that the fence faces be aligned and perpendicular to the tabletop. To check alignment, span the faces with a metal straightedge (bottom photo). There should be no gaps on either side. If there are, add or remove shims between the faces and the fence body until they align. Check for perpendicular with a try square. To adjust, shim the fence or resurface the offending fence face.

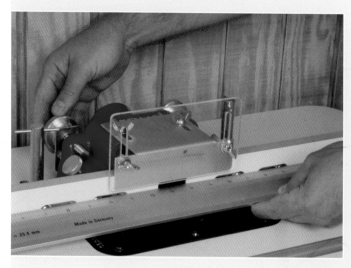

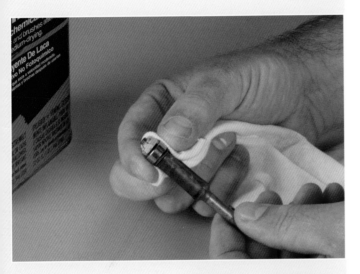

Router Bits

Both HSS (high-speed steel) and carbide-tipped router bits can be tuned up in the shop with a little care and patience. To inspect the cutting edges of the bit, hold it under a bright light (preferably sunlight). If you see a reflection on the edge, the bit is dull.

Bearings

The bearings of bearing-guided bits often become coated with gunk (pitch and gum) and in the case of the flush-trim bit in the top photo, contact cement from trimming a laminated countertop. A rag dipped in acetone or lacquer thinner can remove this. Just take care not to let any solvent creep into the bearing itself, where it can dissolve the bearing grease. For extra insurance, first remove the bearing prior to cleaning (see below).

Shank

The shaft or shank of a router bit will often get beat up over time. If burrs form, file them off with a flat, smooth mill file. Keep the shank in prime shape by periodically scrubbing away any rust or buildup with an abrasive pad (middle photo). Fold the pad in half, squeeze it over the shank, and then rotate the bit while sliding it up and down as shown here.

Remove bearing for cleaning

In order to clean or sharpen a bearing-guided bit properly, the first thing to do is to remove the bearing. For cleaning, this prevents the solvent from dissolving the grease inside the bearing. For sharpening, removing the bearing creates better access for the diamond hone (see page 174). Most bearings are held in place with a hex-head screw and can be removed easily with an Allen wrench. Set these small parts aside in a separate cup or dish — they're easy to misplace.

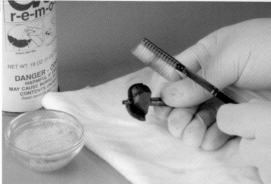

Cleaning router bits

Saw blade cleaner (pitch and gum remover) works great for cleaning router bits. Just make sure that you don't spray it onto a bearing-guided bit, as the cleaner will dissolve the grease in the bearing. Instead, first remove the bearing (see page 173). Since bits are small, it's best to apply the cleaner by first spraying it into a small dish and then applying it with a toothbrush. Let the cleaner rest the recommended time and then scrub it with the brush (top photo). Wipe off any excess and completely dry the bit with a clean, soft cloth.

Sharpening a bit

Use a small, flat, paddle-type diamond hone to sharpen bits. Gently rub the diamond paddle back and forth on the flat face. No lubricant is needed, but a drop of water will help keep the surface from clogging up with fine metal filings. For single-edged bits (like straight bits), continue rubbing until no light is reflected on the edge. For double-edged bits (like round-over bits), take the same number of strokes on each flat face to keep the bit balanced.

What not to sharpen

The secret to successful bit sharpening is to identify which edge to sharpen. Avoid the profiled edge, and sharpen only the flat face of the cutting edge, or you'll change the bit's profile.

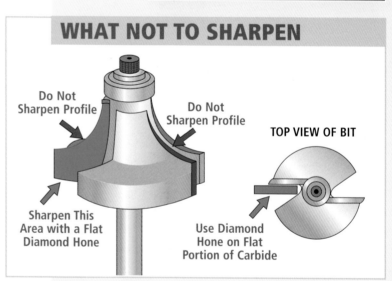

WHAT NOT TO SHARPEN

Do Not Sharpen Profile

Do Not Sharpen Profile

Sharpen This Area with a Flat Diamond Hone

TOP VIEW OF BIT

Use Diamond Hone on Flat Portion of Carbide

DIAMOND HONES

Diamond hones and files are basically pieces of high-grade plastic with crushed industrial-quality diamond particles bonded to the surface. Many shapes and sizes are available, and they typically come in fine, medium, and coarse grits. There are two things that make these terrific. First, since the abrasive is diamond, it lasts a long time. Second, their diminutive size allows them to reach places other stones can't, such as flats of a router bit. Diamond hones and files can be used dry or with water as a lubricant. Since you're usually removing only a small amount of metal with one of these, a lubricant typically is unnecessary.

■ TROUBLESHOOTING

In addition to burning and tear-out (covered on pages 49 and 54–55, respectively), there are two other common routing problems you're likely to encounter: bearing tracks and stepped cuts.

Bearing tracks. Those annoying little tracks on the side of a workpiece (top photo) are caused by pressing the bearing into the edge of the workpiece. The solution is to keep the bearing away from the edge. On a portable router, this can be done by using an edge guide that's adjusted flush with the front of the bearing (left middle photo). With a router table, use a fence adjusted flush with the

front of the bearing (right middle photo). In either case, the additional support prevents the bearing from contacting the edge of the workpiece and causing an indent.

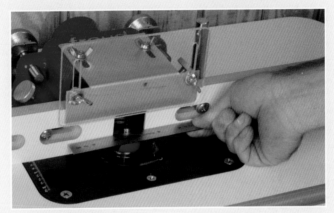

Stepped cuts. Whenever you take more than one pass with a router bit, you run the risk of creating a stepped cut where the two cuts don't align (inset). Stepped cuts on the router table are usually caused by a fence that's not perpendicular to the tabletop (left bottom photo). For a way to fix this, see page 172. On a portable router, stepped cuts can be caused by rotating the router when you make a cut using a straightedge as a guide. To correct this, make a reference mark (see page 168) and keep this against the straightedge as you rout (right bottom photo).

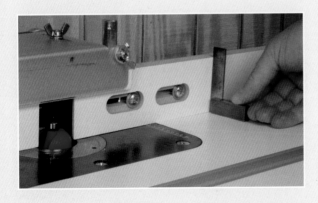

7 Router Projects

The versatility of the router is unmatched by any other power tool. Simply by changing bits you can go from cutting perfect dovetails to pattern-routing matching parts. In fact, many projects can be completely crafted with just a router.

To showcase just some of the tricks you can teach your router to perform, this chapter features four quick and easy projects: a desk clock, a keepsake box, built-up picture frames, and a routed trivet. Each uses a different technique to help you build your skill level. Techniques include pattern-routing, using a router pin arm to rout accurate recesses, making built-up moldings for frames, and using spacers on the router table to create precise matching grooves for a trivet.

Additionally, each of these projects is well suited for production runs — that is, making multiple projects at the same time. Once you've created the templates and set up the router or router table, it takes only a little additional effort to create batches of these projects. Any of these would work well for birthdays, holidays, housewarmings—you get the idea. It's always nice to have a "bank" of completed projects on hand for that special occasion.

Both of the router projects shown here — the desk clock and the keepsake box — use templates to create accurate recesses: one for accepting a clock movement, the other for storing treasures. The clock recess is pattern-routed; the box recesses are made using a pin arm on the router table.

Desk Clock

Simple yet elegant, this desk clock is easy to make in batches with the aid of a template for routing the recess for the clock insert. We used a $2^{3}/_{4}$" extra-thin quartz insert from Klockit (www.klockit.com) for the movement. This movement requires a $2^{3}/_{8}$"-diameter recess that's a minimum of $^{5}/_{8}$" deep, but you can use almost any small quartz insert that's less than 3" in diameter. The desk clock consists of five parts: a body, a top and bottom, and a pair of feet (see the Exploded View at right). The clock insert fits into a recess routed into the body by way of a template and a patternmaker's bit. Because of its small size, this clock is an excellent scrap-wood project. Although we used mahogany, any wood will do. Using the material list below, start by cutting the parts to size.

MATERIALS LIST

Part	Quantity	Dimensions
Body	1	$4^{1}/_{2}$" $\times$ 6" – $1^{3}/_{4}$"
Top	1	$2^{3}/_{4}$" $\times$ $5^{1}/_{2}$" – $^{3}/_{4}$"
Base	1	$2^{3}/_{4}$" $\times$ $5^{1}/_{2}$" – $^{3}/_{4}$"
Feet	2	$1^{1}/_{4}$" $\times$ $3^{1}/_{4}$" – $^{3}/_{8}$"

Bits required

$^{1}/_{2}$" patternmaker's bit
$^{1}/_{2}$" cove bit
$^{1}/_{4}$" cove bit
$^{1}/_{8}$" round-over bit
$^{3}/_{8}$" round-over bit

EXPLODED VIEW

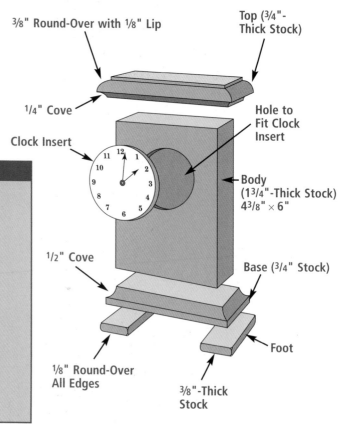

$^{3}/_{8}$" Round-Over with $^{1}/_{8}$" Lip

Top ($^{3}/_{4}$"-Thick Stock)

$^{1}/_{4}$" Cove

Clock Insert

Hole to Fit Clock Insert

Body ($1^{3}/_{4}$"-Thick Stock) $4^{3}/_{8}$" $\times$ 6"

$^{1}/_{2}$" Cove

Base ($^{3}/_{4}$" Stock)

Foot

$^{1}/_{8}$" Round-Over All Edges

$^{3}/_{8}$"-Thick Stock

Make template

The only tricky part to making the desk clock is sizing and routing the insert in the body for the movement. A patternmaker's bit works great for this: You just drill a hole in the template top to match the size of the movement. (Alternatively, you can use a guide bushing and a straight bit, but you'll need to size the template opening larger to compensate for the guide bushing; see page 35 for more on guide bushings.) In most cases, you'll need an adjustable circle cutter to cut the template opening, since hole saws are available only in set increments. The template we made is a 4" × 6" double layer of $1/2$" MDF glued together, but you could also use $1/2$" plywood. The $2^3/8$"-diameter hole is centered on the template and located $2^1/8$" down from the top. After the hole is drilled, attach $2^1/2$"-wide strips of $1/8$" hardboard to the side of the template. These strips have enough flex to allow you to slip the template over the body, yet still hold the template firmly to the body for routing.

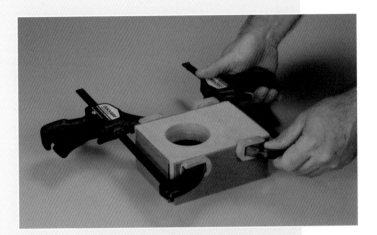

Rout recess

With the template pressed firmly onto the body, set the body on a router pad and adjust your pattern-maker's bit for a $3/16$"-deep cut. Turn the router on and set its base on the template so the bit plunges into the body at the center of the opening (middle photo). Move the router in increasingly larger circles to rout the recess until the bearing of the bit rubs up against the template. Because of the small size of the recess, you'll need to stop frequently to clear out chips. Make sure to stop the router before removing it from the recess to prevent damage to the template. Adjust the bit to take off another $1/8$" to $3/16$" and continue until the desired depth is reached.

Rout cove on base

With the body complete, you can work on the top and bottom. Rout a $1/2$" cove on the top edges of the base (bottom photo). Place the top on a router pad and rout the cove in a series of light passes, increasing the depth of cut as you go. To prevent chip-out, rout the ends first, and then come back and rout the sides.

Rout profiles on top

The top has a pair of profiles: a $3/8$" round-over with a $1/8$" relief on top and a $1/4$" cove on the bottom. To provide the maximum surface for the router bearings, first rout the $1/4$" cove — two passes will do. Then switch to the round-over bit and take three passes, ending up with a full round-over and a $1/8$" relief (top photo). You'll want to rout the ends first, then the sides.

Finish the feet

The last routing task is to soften all the edges of the feet — top, bottom, ends, and sides — with a $1/8$" round-over bit. Although you could do this with sandpaper, you'll get a much more uniform edge with the round-over bit. Because the feet are so thin, you'll need to stack them on top of each other to keep the bit's bearing from contacting the router pad (middle photo). The safest way to rout small parts like this is to temporarily fasten them to each other and then to a piece of scrap wood with double-sided carpet tape.

Assemble the clock

Before assembling the clock, first sand all parts to the desired smoothness. Then center the base onto the bottom of the body and secure it with #8 × 2" flathead woodscrews. Next, attach the feet to the base with #6 × $3/4$" flathead woodscrews. The feet are centered from front to back and extend out from the sides of the body $5/16$". Finally, attach the top with glue only, and clamp it in place until the glue dries (bottom photo). Alternatively, drill counterbored holes, attach with screws, and fill the holes with matching wood plugs. All that's left is to apply a finish and, when dry, add the movement.

Keepsake Box

This unique keepsake box can store jewelry, mementos, almost any treasure. A pair of hinged lids swivel out to provide access to two deep recesses routed into the body of the box. The hinges are simply short lengths of dowel set into the body and the lid. The lids are hinged at opposite ends so they can swivel open — something that wouldn't be possible if they were hinged at the same end. The recesses in the body are routed using a pin arm on the router table, but you could also rout them with a template and either a patternmaker's bit or a straight bit and a guide bushing. After you rout the recess, the box and lid parts can be cut into a circle with a band saw or saber saw and sanded smooth (as shown here), or you could rout them round with the small circle-cutting jig shown on page 139.

EXPLODED VIEW

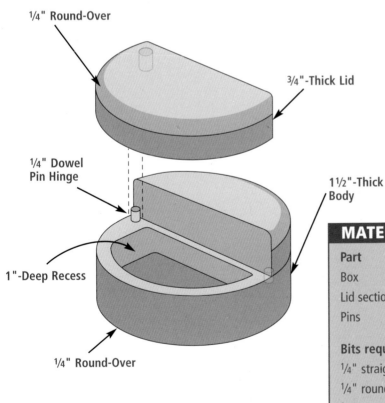

1/4" Round-Over

3/4"-Thick Lid

1/4" Dowel Pin Hinge

1 1/2"-Thick Body

1"-Deep Recess

1/4" Round-Over

MATERIALS LIST

Part	Quantity	Dimensions
Box	1	5" × 5" – 1 1/2"
Lid sections	2	2 1/2" × 5" – 5/8"
Pins	2	1"-long, 1/4" dowels

Bits required
1/4" straight bit
1/4" round-over bit
1/8" round-over bit

Make the template

The template we used to rout the recesses is designed for a router pin arm, shown below. If you plan to use a patternmaker's bit or a straight bit and a guide bushing, you'll need to alter the template accordingly. Our template is a $5^1/2$" square of $^1/4$" plywood. To make it, start by locating the center and then scribing 5"- and $4^1/2$"-diameter circles. The smaller circle defines the recess; the outer circle is the outside wall of the box. Next, mark a $^1/4$"-wide centered

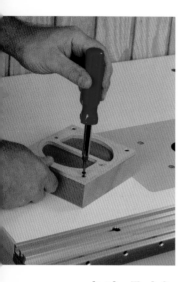

divider. To define the areas where the hinge pins will be installed, measure down $^1/2$" from the inner circle at opposite ends of the divider and draw a perpendicular line. Lay out the hinge pin holes by measuring $^1/4$" in from the center divider and $^1/4$" down from the inner circle — drill $^1/4$" holes in the template. Now you can drill an access hole in each recess and cut out the opening with a coping saw, saber saw, or scroll saw. Sand the inside edges smooth and then attach the template to the body blank with screws at each corner, as shown in the photo above.

Rout recesses

Set up the pin arm on the router table (see page 127 for more on this), and insert a $^1/4$" straight bit into the router. Set the bit height for a $^1/4$"-deep cut, and begin routing the recesses. Lift the pin arm and position the pin inside one of the openings in the template. Turn on the router and lower the box onto the bit. Tighten the lock knob on the pin arm, and move the box in gentle circles until the pin rubs up against the template and all the waste has been removed. Stop the router, lift the pin arm, and rout the other recess. Repeat this procedure, raising the bit in $^1/4$" increments until the desired depth is achieved; we stopped at 1" (see the photo).

PIN ARM DETAIL

The pin arm shown in the drawing at right attaches to the top of the router table via a set of clamps — it's designed for routing $1^1/2$"-thick stock. The pin arm consists of three parts: a 1"-thick base made of a double layer of $^1/4$" MDF or plywood, a $^3/4$"-thick top, and a $^3/8$" clear acrylic arm that holds the metal pin. The

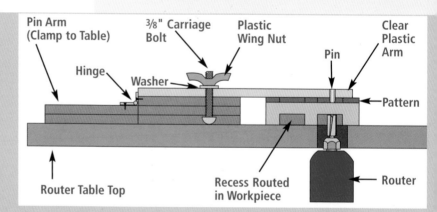

top attaches to the base via a 3"-wide hinge and a $^3/8$" carriage bolt and plastic wing nut. The base is $3^1/2$" × 12", the top is $3^1/2$" × 7", and the arm is $3^1/2$" × 12". The metal pin is centered on the arm and is $2^1/4$" in from the front edge. The pin is just a $^1/2$"-long piece of $^1/4$" metal rod with the ends filed smooth; it's epoxied into the hole drilled into the clear plastic arm.

Drill hinge pin holes

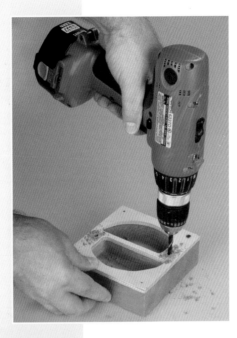

Before you cut or rout the box to shape, it's best to drill the holes for the hinge pins. Since the template creates a mirror image of the recesses on the bottom of the box, you'll need to remove the template, flip it over, and reattach it to the box as shown in the top photo. With a 1/4" bit, drill 1/2"-deep holes through the template and into the box. Use the template to mark and drill matching holes in the lid pieces once they've been cut to size.

Cut or rout shape

Once the hinge pin holes have been drilled, you can cut the box into a circle (alternatively, you could leave it square). Cut the circle out with a saber saw or band saw, or rout it into a perfect circle with the circle-cutting jig shown on page 139. Next, cut the lid pieces to shape to match the diameter of the box, and smooth the edges of the box and lids with sandpaper.

Round over edges

All that's left is to soften the edges of the box and lids. A 1/4" round-over bit fitted in a laminate trimmer works great (bottom photo). Round over only the *bottom* of the box and the *top* edges of the lids. You can also run a 1/8" round-over bit along the inside edges of the recesses to soften them as well. Finally, apply a finish to all the parts and, when dry, add the hinge pins and attach the lids.

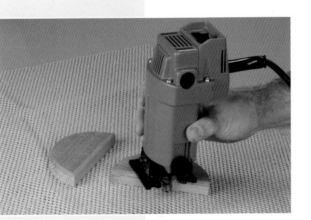

Picture Frames

Here are two picture frames that each use a simple technique called "built-up" moldings. Basically, the edges of separate pieces are routed to create decorative effects. Then they're glued together, or "built up," to create a much richer, visually interesting frame that you can't get from a single piece of wood. Finally, these strips are mitered to form a frame of any size. A tight-grained hardwood works best for the frames. If you want to get creative, you can use different woods to build up the molding. Cherry and walnut work well together, as do cherry and maple. Routing thin strips of wood like this is best done on the router table, where you'll have more control of the workpiece.

The number and length of the strips you'll need depends on the size of the object you're framing. Lengths over 3 feet get cumbersome. Note: Always make a couple of extra strips as insurance. As a general rule of thumb, measure your object and add 10" to both the length and width of each side to determine the minimum lengths you'll need. Since you're going to the trouble of cutting wood and making the router table setups, it's well worth the time to make enough molding for at least one more frame.

Rout profiles on first piece

All of the routing takes place at the router table, or a table-mounted router. Although the full profile cut is shown in the illustrations, it's always safer taking multiple passes — usually three light cuts to sneak up on the final profile. This is especially important when working with thin or narrow strips. It's also a good idea to rig up a featherboard or hold-down to press the strip firmly against the router fence during routing. The 1/8" round-over with a 1/8" relief is routed on its edge, as shown in step 1 of Frame #1. For added

stability, consider clamping a support strip to this piece to prevent it from tipping during routing.

Rout profiles on trim

The trim pieces for both frames shown here use thin stock. Your best bet for holding these safely for routing is an ordinary grout float, like the one shown below. The float's rubber face will grip the piece firmly; even if a slip occurs, at worst the bit will cut into the rubber face. When routing a full round-over (such as two 1/8" round-overs on 1/4"-thick stock), it's best to use a fence for the second pass: The first pass will remove the edge that the bearing would normally ride along.

MATERIALS LIST

Part	Quantity	Dimensions
FRAME #1		
Body	1	3/4" × 1 1/4" – to length
Trim	1	1/4" × 3/4" – to length
FRAME #2		
Body	1	3/4" × 2" – to length
Middle trim	1	1/2" × 1/2" – to length
Top trim	1	1/4" × 1 1/8" – to length

Bits required

FRAME #1	1/8" round-over bit
	1/2" straight bit or 3/8" rabbeting bit
	1/2" core-box or cove bit
FRAME #2	1/8" round-over bit
	1/2" round-over bit
	1/2" straight bit or 3/8" rabbeting bit
	1/2" core-box or cove bit

Rout rabbet

With all the profiles routed, rout a rabbet on the inside edge to accept the picture. Rout this in a series of light passes to prevent tear-out. You can do this either with a rabbeting bit or with a straight bit and a fence, as shown in the drawings. A $3/8$"-deep rabbet will allow for a picture, glass, and backing.

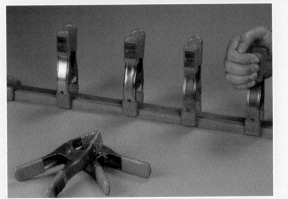

Glue pieces together

Once the strips have been routed, they can be glued together. Two critical things to note: First, it's important that the back edges of the strip be flush. Second, apply glue sparingly so you don't get squeeze-out at the joint, where you'd have to scrape it off. Clamp the two pieces together, making sure the back edges are flush (spring clamps work great for this, but you'll need a lot; they're relatively inexpensive). Tip: You can make inexpensive clamps by cutting long strips from an inner tube. Just stretch and wrap a strip around the molding, applying tension as you wrap.

FRAME #1 DETAIL

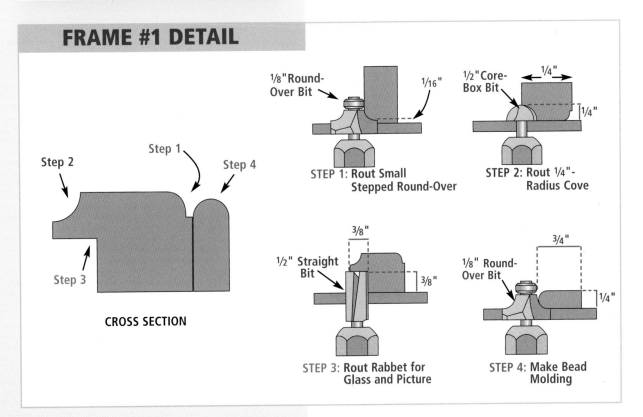

Step 2   Step 1   Step 4

Step 3

CROSS SECTION

$1/8$" Round-Over Bit $1/16$"

STEP 1: Rout Small Stepped Round-Over

$1/2$" Core-Box Bit $1/4$" $1/4$"

STEP 2: Rout $1/4$"-Radius Cove

$3/8$" $1/2$" Straight Bit $3/8$"

STEP 3: Rout Rabbet for Glass and Picture

$3/4$" $1/8$" Round-Over Bit $1/4$"

STEP 4: Make Bead Molding

Glue up frame

After you've miter-cut the pieces to the desired length, start by gluing up pairs of adjacent sides. Apply glue to both ends and butt the pieces up against the small plywood square — this ensures that they'll glue up at 90 degrees. Hold the pieces in place with hand pressure for 2 minutes, then let them dry overnight. After you've glued up the two pairs, glue these together, pressing the joints at the same time; a band clamp like the one shown here works great for this. For larger frames, reinforce the joints by lock-nailing them after the glue has set overnight. Drill a small hole in from the top and bottom at each joint, then drive in a finish nail. For heavy frames, add a metal mending plate across each joint for reinforcement.

Add backing

With the frame complete, sand it to the desired smoothness and apply a finish to the frame (spray polyurethane works well). If you're mounting a picture, cut glass and a back ($1/8$" or $1/4$", depending on the glass thickness) to fit; secure the picture, glass, and back in the frame with glazier's points. Add hangers and picture wire after you've mounted the back.

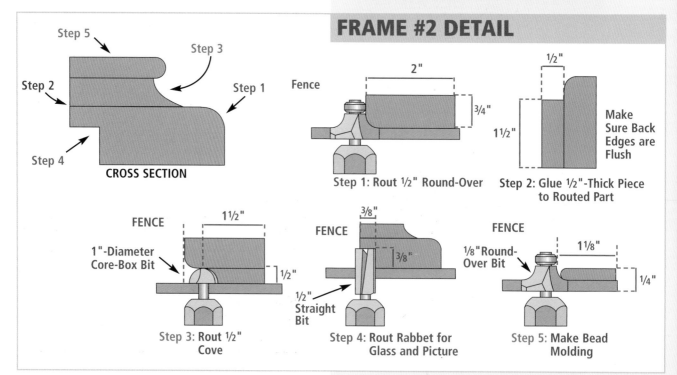

FRAME #2 DETAIL

Step 5 · Step 3 · Step 2 · Step 1 · Step 4

CROSS SECTION

Fence — 2" — 3/4"
Step 1: Rout 1/2" Round-Over

1/2" · 1 1/2" · Make Sure Back Edges are Flush
Step 2: Glue 1/2"-Thick Piece to Routed Part

FENCE — 1 1/2" — 1"-Diameter Core-Box Bit — 1/2"
Step 3: Rout 1/2" Cove

FENCE — 3/8" — 3/8" — 1/2" Straight Bit
Step 4: Rout Rabbet for Glass and Picture

FENCE — 1/8" Round-Over Bit — 1 1/8" — 1/4"
Step 5: Make Bead Molding

Routed Trivet

Whether it's protecting a tabletop from a hot casserole or a counter from a pot of tea, this routed trivet will get the job done with style. The precisely spaced grooves are created using spacers and a double stop fence arrangement on the router table. The same spacers are used to make the crisscross pattern — the wood is simply rotated 90 degrees after each pass. Also, you can rout grooves in one direction only, and if desired, rout both faces of the trivet or just one face.

Almost any wood will work for this as long, as it's flat. Although the trivet shown here is 7" square, you can make it any size in 1" increments. As with many router table projects, once you've gone to the trouble to set up the fences and spacers, you might as well make a couple extra of these. They make great gifts.

When complete, the trivet can be unfinished or finished. To finish it, wipe on a few coats of mineral oil and let each coat soak in fully before applying the next. Wipe off any excess oil, and allow the trivet to dry a couple of days. Then buff the surface vigorously with a clean, soft cloth to bring up a soft luster.

TRIVET DETAIL

CROSS SECTION

MATERIALS LIST

Part	Quantity	Dimensions
Trivet	1	7" × 7" – ³/₄"

Bits required

¹/₄" round-over bit

¹/₂" core-box bit

Position fences

The instructions that follow are for the 7" square trivet shown here, with grooves spaced 1" apart and 1" in from the sides. You'll need to cut five spacers to a width of 1" and $1\frac{7}{8}$" long. The simplest way to set up the fences is to start by positioning the router table fence 6" away from the center of the core-box bit. Then clamp a stop fence on each side and perpendicular to the router table fence, as shown. Each of these fences is located 6" from the center of the bit. This will create a 12" space from fence to fence. Since the spacers are $1\frac{7}{8}$" long, there's $\frac{1}{8}$" of clearance to allow the spacers to be removed without binding on the sides of the stop fences.

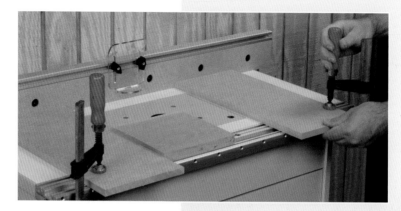

Set up spacers

The advantage of using spacers is that you don't have to reposition the fence after every groove is routed. Additionally, the spacers will guarantee accurate spacing, as long as they're all cut to the same width. To set up for routing the grooves, start by placing all five of the spacers between the bit and the router table fence. Then butt them all firmly up against the fence. As you rout grooves, you'll remove the spacers one at a time.

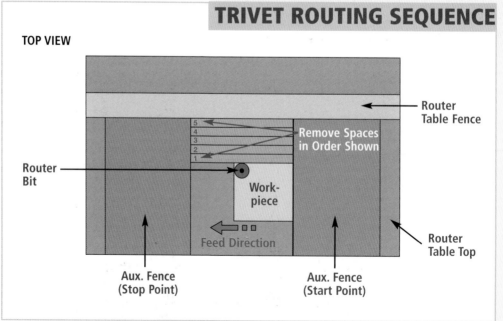

TRIVET ROUTING SEQUENCE

TOP VIEW

Router Table Fence

Remove Spaces in Order Shown

5
4
3
2
1

Router Bit

Work-piece

Feed Direction

Aux. Fence (Stop Point)

Aux. Fence (Start Point)

Router Table Top

Rout grooves in one direction

Now you're ready to rout. Start by setting the core-box bit for a $1/8$"-deep cut so you can complete each groove in two passes. Turn the router on and, holding the trivet blank at an angle, butt the right edge of the trivet up against the right stop fence. Then gently lower the blank onto the bit. As soon as the blank is flat on the table, begin pushing the trivet from right to left. Make sure to keep solid pressure against the spacers. When the left edge of the trivet blank butts up against the left stop fence, raise the right edge up off the table. If you hesitate anywhere along the line, you'll likely leave a burn mark. If the groove is routed in one fluid motion, you'll get a clean groove with very little burning. It's a good idea to practice this drop, push, and lift motion on some scrap until it feels comfortable, before using your good stock.

Rout perpendicular grooves

After you've routed the groove on one side, flip the trivet blank over and rout a matching groove on the opposite face. Then rotate the blank 90 degrees and rout a groove perpendicular to the first groove. Do this on the opposite face as well. Now remove the first spacer and repeat for the second set of grooves. Continue removing spacers and routing grooves until all are complete. Then raise the bit up another $1/8$" and repeat this entire process, starting with all the spacers in place.

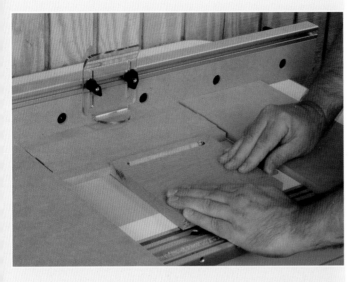

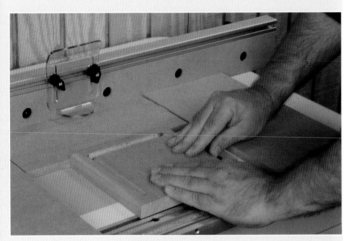

Round over edges

Once all the grooves have been routed, you can round over the edges. If desired, first round over the corners by marking a $3/8$" radius and removing the waste with a saw. Sand the corners smooth and round over all edges with a $1/4$" round-over bit. Tip: If there are any burn marks, remove the bit from the router and use it as a tiny scraper — it's a perfect fit for the groove.

INDEX

A

Accessories. *See also* Bits
  for handheld routers,
    34–35
  for table-mounted routers,
    39–43
Air-powered routers, 13
Amperage ratings, 15
Anti-kickback bits, 26
Auxiliary fences
  for edge guides, 62
  for table-mounted routers,
    93, 94

B

Backer boards
  for dadoes, 98
  for decorative profiles, 121
  for lap joints, 113
  for tenons, 107
Backrouting
  with handheld routers, 56
  with table-mounted routers
    caution against, 88
    to prevent chip-out,
      101, 121
Base, described, 164
Base plates
  maintenance of, 168
  oversized, 58, 133–135
Beading bits
  non-piloted, 31
  piloted, 28
Bearing-guided bits, 27, 173
Bearing tracks, 175
Bit guards, 41
Bit-height adjustments
  cleaning and maintenance
    of, 165, 171
  on handheld routers,
    17, 18, 50
  jig for, 51
  on table-mounted routers,
    89
Bits
  anti-kickback, 26
  bearing- vs. non-bearing-
    guided, 27
  cabinet for, shop-made,
    140–143
  changing, 19
  cleaning and maintenance
    of, 173–174
  design of, 25

high-speed steel (HSS) vs.
    carbide, 24
  installing in collet, 14
  interchangeable arbors
    for, 25
  piloted vs. non-piloted, 27
  profiles of
    non-piloted, 30–31
    piloted, 28–29, 79
    specialty, 32–33, 102
  sharpening, 174
  size of, 24
Box joints
  cutting, 114–115
  jigs for, 45, 144–148
Brushes, replacing, 170
Built-up moldings, 184–186
Burning, 49
Burrs, removing
  on base plates, 168
  on bits, 173
  on collets, 166–167
  on collet wrenches, 167
Bushing sets, 35

C

Cabinet, for router bits,
  140–143
Carbide bits, 24
Chamfer bits, 29
Chamfer cuts, 59
Chattering, 24, 49
Chip-out and tear-out
  on dadoes, 98, 99
  on decorative profiles, 121
  described, 54
  on lap joints, 113
  preventing, 55
  on rabbets, 101
  on tenons, 107
Chisels
  rounding tenons with, 109
  squaring mortises with,
    106
Circle jigs
  described, 44
  making, 136–139
  using, 138
Clamps. *See also specific cuts*
  for backrouting, 56
  for holding small pieces,
    95
  safety and, 57
Classic pattern bits
  non-piloted, 31

  piloted, 29
Cleaning routers, 165. *See also*
  Maintenance; *specific parts*
Clock project, 178–180
Collar-and-groove height
  adjustments, 17, 50
Collet nuts, 167
Collets
  cleaning and maintenance
    of, 165, 166–167
  installing bits in, 14
  types and sizes of, 14
Collet wrenches, 167
Cope-and-stick bit sets, 32
Cope-and-stick joints,
  116–117
Cordless routers, 11
Cords, replacing, 169
Core-box bits, 30
Corner chisels, 106
Cove bits, 28
Cuts. *See also specific cuts
  or joints*
    guided, 60–62
    piloted, 59, 91
    stabilizing, 52–53
    stepped, 175
    stopped, 63

D

Dadoes
  cutting, 60, 98–99
  defined, 60
Decorative profiles
  bits for, 33
  cutting
    with handheld routers,
      59
    with table-mounted
      routers, 120
    preventing chip-out on,
      121
Depth of cut. *See* Bit-height
  adjustments
Depth stops, 50
Desk clock project, 178–180
Diamond hones, 174
Dovetail bits, 31
Dovetails
  cutting, 72–77
  jigs for, 44
Dowels, making, 124–125
Dremel routers, 13
Dual-base routers, 11
Duplicating parts, 79, 127

Dust collection
  accessories for, 35, 41
  safety and, 57

E

Ear protection, 57
Edge-beading bits, 29
Edge grain, routing profiles
  on, 120
Edge guides
  described, 34
  using, 62
Edge mold bits, 31
Edging strips, trimming, 78
Electrical repairs, 169–170
End grain
  chip-out and, 121
  routing profiles on, 120
Ergonomics, 16
Exploded view of router, 164
Eye protection, 57

F

Feed direction
  for handheld routers, 48
  for table-mounted routers,
    88
Feed rate
  for handheld routers, 49
  for table-mounted routers,
    88
Fence-guided sleds, 43
Fences
  for edge guides, 62
  for handheld routers, 52
  for table-mounted routers
    auxiliary, 93, 94
    described, 39
    maintenance of, 172
    making, 94, 156–161
    using, 92–94
Fence stops, 40
Finger joints (box joints)
  cutting, 114–115
  jigs for, 45, 144–148
Fixed-base routers. *See also
  specific cuts or techniques*
  adjustments on, 17, 50
  basic techniques for,
    48–55
  brand comparisons, 20
  described, 8–9
  exploded view of, 164
  holding, 48
  reasons to buy, 20